RULES OF
DISENGAGEMENT

RULES OF DISENGAGEMENT

The Politics and Honor of Military Dissent

MARJORIE COHN and
KATHLEEN GILBERD

 PoliPointPress

Rules of Disengagement: The Politics and Honor of Military Dissent

Copyright © 2009 by Marjorie Cohn and Kathleen Gilberd

13   12   11   10   09   1   2   3   4   5

Production management: BookMatters
Book design: BookMatters
Cover design: Lisa Fyfe

Library of Congress Cataloging-in-Publication Data
   Cohn, Marjorie, 1948–
      Rules of disengagement : the politics and honor of military dissent / Marjorie Cohn and Kathleen Gilberd.
         p.   cm.
   Includes index.
   ISBN 978-0-9815769-2-3
   1. Conscientious objection—United States.
   2. Military ethics—United States.
   3. War—Moral and ethical aspects—United States.
   4. Vietnam War, 1961–1975—Moral and ethical aspects.
   5. Afghan War, 2001—Moral and ethical aspects.
   6. Iraq War, 2003—Moral and ethical aspects.
   7. Soldiers—Legal status, laws, etc.—United States.
   I. Gilberd, Kathleen.   II. Title.
   U22.C542   2009
   172'.42—dc22   2009004870

Published by:
PoliPointPress, LLC
P.O. Box 3008
Sausalito, CA 94966-3008
(415) 339-4100
www.p3books.com
Distributed by Ingram Publisher Services

Printed in the USA

Contents

To my father, Leonard Cohn,
and my husband, Jerry Wallingford,
both veterans for peace
—MC

To Terry Christian, whose compassion
and lifelong commitment to activism
continue to inspire
—KG

Introduction

RULES OF ENGAGEMENT limit forms of combat, levels of force, and legitimate enemy targets, defining what is legal in warfare and what is not. In the modern world, the rules of engagement are defined by an established body of international law and, for American soldiers, by U.S. law as well.

When the government at the highest levels ignores these rules, when the conduct of a war and the war itself violate the law, as happened in Vietnam and is now happening in Iraq and Afghanistan, soldiers are forced into a legal and ethical dilemma. They must decide whether to abide by law and conscience—knowing the government does not—or to follow orders without regard to the law.

Rules of Disengagement examines the legal and moral questions posed by these wars through the eyes of American soldiers, showing the effects the wars have had on the soldiers' lives and those of their families. Chapters 1 and 2 address the legality and morality of the Iraq and Afghanistan wars in the words of soldiers and sailors who oppose those conflicts. Chapter 3 examines the recent Winter Soldier Investigation, where veterans and service members testified about extensive violations of the rules of engagement in both theaters of combat. In each chapter, we explore the frightening parallels to the war in Vietnam, again using the words and experiences of veterans of that war.

Chapters 5 through 7 and Chapter 9 analyze the relationship between the military mission—the conduct of these illegal wars—and the conditions under which soldiers live and serve. They discuss the effect of illegal warfare on such concrete matters as medical care, racial discrimination, and violence against women in the military, and they examine frightening similarities to soldiers' experiences during the Vietnam War. Chapter 9 considers briefly the effects of the wars on military families and the ways in which families, too, have fought back. In Chapter 4 and again in Chapter 8, we describe the ways soldiers have chosen to disengage from these wars, and we discuss their rights under military law and regulations. That practical discussion appears throughout the book, because our work with service members has shown us that GIs are not just asking questions—they are also looking for practical ways to address their concerns.

Many parallels are discernible between the war in Vietnam and the wars in Iraq and Afghanistan. During the Vietnam War, American troops operated in "free-fire zones." John Kerry told Congress in 1971, "We learned the meaning of free-fire zones, shooting anything that moves, and we watched while America placed a cheapness on the lives of Orientals."[1]

Veterans of the Iraq war testified at the March 2008 Winter Soldier hearings that they were subject to vague and ever-changing rules of engagement—often free-fire zones. This vagueness led to confusion and the commission of atrocities, many of which would constitute war crimes in violation of the Geneva Conventions and the U.S. War Crimes Act.[2] "We killed so many innocent people," said Ivan Medina, an Army chaplain's assistant in Iraq. "They said if it moves, you shoot."[3] Just as soldiers during Vietnam were taught to think of all Vietnamese as the enemy, troops in Iraq and Afghanistan have been trained to consider all Iraqis and Afghanis as the enemy. This indoctrination has led to massive civilian casualties.

Service members who fought in Vietnam, and recently in Iraq and Afghanistan, have challenged not only the rules under which they operated but also the very propriety of American engagement in those wars. Many have concluded that the wars were illegal because they violated the Charter of the United Nations, a ratified treaty that is part of U.S. law.

Soldiers like Dr. Howard Levy during Vietnam and Pablo Paredes during Operation Iraqi Freedom have raised the Nuremberg defense, which is enshrined in our law and which creates a duty to obey lawful orders and to disobey unlawful orders. An order to fight in an illegal war, they have maintained, is an unlawful order. Other soldiers have professed opposition to all wars and filed for conscientious objector (CO) status. Through these acts of resistance and protest, service members in growing numbers are fighting for disengagement—the disengagement of the U.S. military from Iraq and Afghanistan, their personal disengagement from illegal and immoral orders, and in many cases, their disengagement from the military itself.

Just as soldiers are affected by violations of the rules of engagement by being forced to participate in illegal wars, so the whole military is affected by having to wage such a war. Morale and support for the war affect enlistments and reenlistments. Unable to guarantee a sufficient body of willing combatants, the military presses troops into repeated deployments, using stop-loss policies—presidential orders and implementing regulations that permit the military to keep soldiers on active duty beyond their normal terms of enlisted service—and a variety of other means to keep soldiers in the field. Unable to convince soldiers that they are defending their country and communities, the military turns to other methods of motivating soldiers, using racism to instill hatred of an enemy, to dehumanize a race and religion, and to define a whole population as the enemy. A deliberate dehumanization of women and demeaning, violent sexual imagery become training tools, methods of motivation, and "morale boosters." These methods invariably engender violence against fellow soldiers.

The military as an institution is strained by these illegal wars as well. Illegitimate warfare fractures the military's infrastructure and organization. The need to return soldiers to combat over and over again forces commands to ignore medical problems until they become crises and to deny support to soldiers and their families. Our national military budget emphasizes weapons systems and benefits private contractors rather than funding medical care and support systems. Everything and everyone suffers when the military is forced to focus resources and energy on maintaining the fiction of legitimate and successful wars—no time or resources are available for the military to take care of its own.

In these ways the nature of a military mission affects the conditions of soldiers' day-to-day lives. Poor health care, poor gear, poor safety conditions, poor training, and the use of racist stereotypes and sexism are not inherent in a military—rather, they are inherent in a military fighting illegal and immoral wars and ignoring basic rules of engagement. They are inherent in a military that is required to fight, not against an opposing army or a terrorist band but against a whole people.

Rules of Disengagement explores the many ways in which soldiers have begun to disengage from the wars and the military, again with parallels to the lessons of the Vietnam-era GI movement. Throughout, we discuss the laws and regulations governing military dissent and resistance—the legal rules of disengagement. We offer service members practical guidelines for dissent and disengagement, from political protest to requesting discharge from the service.

The Vietnam-era GI Movement

The similarities between the wars in Iraq and Afghanistan and the war in Vietnam are remarkable and sobering. Although political, technological, and cultural changes create many differences in war and warfare, the questions and dilemmas that soldiers faced in the 1960s and 1970s are strikingly similar to those they have confronted in recent years. So, too, are the decisions of growing numbers of soldiers to disengage from the wars similar to the choices made then.

The number of soldiers and sailors who refused to fight in Vietnam is larger than most people would expect. Many soldiers and sailors sought to be declared conscientious objectors. Many claims were wrongly denied at the local command level and never reported to military headquarters. Rates for other discharges soared as disgruntled service members searched the regulations for ways to get out of the military. Many walked away. The Department of Defense (DoD) estimated that there were 73.5 desertions per 1,000 soldiers from the Army and 56.2 per 1,000 from the Marine Corps in 1971.[4] Over the course of the war, more than 500,000 soldiers deserted. A support network of civilian attorneys and lay people set up military counseling centers around the United States and overseas to provide assistance for GIs seeking discharge or dealing with the legal consequences of desertion. As frustrations rose among the troops, killings of officers by angry enlisted men, known as *fraggings,* occurred at the rate of at least one per week. Colonel Robert Heinl, a military policy analyst, wrote in 1971, "The morale, discipline and battle-worthiness of the U.S. armed forces are, with a few salient exceptions, lower and worse than at any time in this century and possibly in the history of the United States."[5]

Many GIs felt betrayed by their government. All over the United States, in Germany, and in Asia, they established underground newspapers and set up coffeehouses and centers where service members met and discussed politics and strategies for resisting. Quiet opposition turned into a tidal wave of resistance that developed throughout the course of the Vietnam War. Some GIs complained in their churches about what the military was teaching them. Many GIs began to salute trash cans or mail dead fish to particularly loathsome officers. Mass protests were held, and a number of GIs were prosecuted. The draft galvanized the antiwar movement among college students.

"The Nixon administration claimed and received great credit for withdrawing the Army from Vietnam, but it was the rebellion of low-ranking GIs that forced the government to abandon a hopeless suicidal policy," Vietnam War veteran David Cortright wrote in his book *Soldiers in Revolt*.[6] Rebellion among Army soldiers became so strong that the Pentagon consciously shifted its strategy from ground combat to an air war over Indochina, relying on Navy and Air Force resources and personnel.

Sailors and airmen responded by increasing their protests and refusals. Underground newspapers began appearing on Navy ships, and some sailors staged demonstrations onboard. Others joined together in rebellions such as the one on the San Diego–based USS *Constellation* in 1972. There, black sailors formed an organization to protest racial discrimination and poor, unsafe working conditions on aging Navy ships that were pressed into service in repeated deployments. More than 100 black and white sailors staged a sit-in and demanded that the *Constellation*'s commander hear their grievances. One hundred thirty men refused to board the ship.

They held a militant dockside strike, one of the largest acts of mass disobedience in naval history. None of the men were arrested; some received early discharges, and others were reassigned to shore duty. This rebellion and literally hundreds of other protests by black service members were evidence of a new awareness of racism in the military and its relation to the war. African American and white sailors began to discuss the links between racism at home and racism used to instill hatred of the Vietnamese people. In a similar way, women in the military and their civilian supporters began to explore the ways in which sexism was used to train and motivate soldiers, bringing to light serious problems of sexual discrimination, harassment, and abuse in the armed forces.

The *Constellation* incident captured the Pentagon's attention. Chief of Naval Operations Admiral Elmo Zumwalt met with 80 top admirals and Marine Corps generals to discuss the situation. The House Armed Services Committee appointed a special subcommittee to investigate the "discipline problems" in the Navy. The committee concluded that the resistance of the sailors undermined naval combat operations during the 1972 bombing campaign. Resistance in the Air Force also crippled U.S. bombing operations.

Ten years after the United States began bombing Vietnam, the deadly war finally came to an end. It had claimed the lives of 58,000 Americans and 2 million to 3 million Indochinese. The termination of American involvement in Vietnam was largely a result, in addition to the resilience of the North Vietnamese, of the antiwar movement, particularly the resistance by American GIs.

Today's GI Movement

Despite conservative and revisionist histories that speak of the Vietnam War as a failure of will, GIs, veterans, and the public today remember that movement and its symbols—peace signs, raised fists, and broken rifles—on the covers of underground newspapers and on soldiers' helmets in Vietnam. Those symbols were picked up again, and the lessons of the movement were considered during Operation Desert Storm. The energy and strength of the GI anti-war movement has been reflected in service members' peacetime struggles against sexual discrimination and military homophobia in the decades since the Vietnam War.

Now a new generation of GIs and veterans is discussing the examples and lessons of the Vietnam era. Military resistance to the occupation of Iraq and the war in Afghanistan is growing and beginning to have a real impact on the conduct of those wars. Like soldiers and sailors during the Vietnam War, service members today have chosen many forms of resistance and protest, ranging from going absent without leave (AWOL) and refusing orders to publishing newsletters and mounting petition campaigns. Some GIs protest the war while still on active duty. Others seek to get out, often organizing service members to oppose the war once they are no longer in the military. Some speak out peacefully; others engage in militant action. Many GIs seek conscientious objector status, claiming opposition not just to the Iraq war but to all war.

During Vietnam soldiers and sailors were conscripted into the armed forces, whereas today we have an "all-volunteer" military. Many cite this difference when comparing the GI movement in the Vietnam era with resistance to the Iraq and Afghanistan wars. Yet much of the GI resistance to the Vietnam War came from volunteers, not draftees. The majority of dissenters and organizers were enlistees from working-class backgrounds.[7] Young men with money and education had an easier time obtaining student defer-ments, conscientious objector status, and other deferments and exemptions from the draft. "Draftees expect shit, get shit, aren't even disappointed. Volunteers expect something better, get the same shit, and have at least one more year to get mad about it," Jim Goodman wrote in the Baumholder *Gig Sheet*, an underground newspaper produced by GIs in Germany during Vietnam.[8] Today we have a "poverty draft," where the bulk of those who enlist have few options other than joining the military.[9] And the stop-loss program has created a "backdoor draft," which keeps many soldiers in the military involuntarily even after their contracts expire.

As this book goes to press, official counts admit that 4,227 American soldiers, sailors, airmen, and Marines have been killed in Iraq, and 640 have been killed in Afghanistan. The military acknowledges that 31,004 U.S. troops have been wounded in action in Iraq, and 2,679 have been wounded in action in and around Afghanistan.[10] Many more have returned from combat zones with undiagnosed injuries or illness. Over 1 million Iraqis have been killed.

More than 1.6 million men and women have served in Iraq, Afghanistan, or both since October 2001. Deployments have grown longer, redeployment to combat zones has been common, and breaks between deployments are inadequate.

Soldiers, their families, veterans, and civilians around the country see rising death and injury tolls, news reports of atrocities and brutality in combat areas, and "victories" that evaporate overnight. They hear warnings about "perpetual war," and "a long struggle" against some vague enemy, and they learn about legal experts and foreign officials who challenge the wars as illegal. These experiences raise questions for all service members and civilians: do we have a duty to carry out the wars and support them at home, or a duty to resist?

From the Vietnam War to the present, dissident soldiers have spoken out in opposition to illegitimate wars and in doing so have expanded soldiers' right to dissent. Their legal challenges and political efforts have broadened the rights of other service members opposed to a war or oppressive military policies. Continued protests and legal challenges to repression of dissenting GIs have forced the military to acknowledge service members' limited constitutional protections of free speech and association. Dissent has increased the rights of soldiers and sailors to sign petitions, speak with their congressional representatives, join public protests, and engage in other political action.

In spite of a traditionally conservative military leadership, the right to dissent in the military is much more extensive than soldiers and their families are told. As soldiers continue to resist the wars, military racism and sexual harassment, denial of proper medical care, and other destructive practices, they act in an honorable tradition and pave the way for military protesters who will come after them. Those who protest the current wars in Iraq and Afghanistan follow in the footsteps of military personnel from the Vietnam era, renewing old methods of dissent, from petitions and public letters to demonstrations and picket lines. At the same time, brave and outspoken service members create new and innovative forms of dissent: blogging, sharing photos and videos of the brutal reality on the ground in Iraq and Afghanistan through the Internet, and developing new ways to speak out to fellow soldiers and civilians online and in the media.

We now have a military full of soldiers who are Internet savvy and used to long-distance exchange of information and ideas. Although the military controls much of the official flow of news from Iraq and Afghanistan, GIs share information that gives the public a real sense of the war, often through digital images of prisoner abuse; the destruction of homes, neighborhoods, and lives in Iraq; and coffins returning to the United States. In some ways these messages are individual and isolated, but they can reach many more people than letters and photographs sent home from Vietnam. As the new movement has grown, it has picked up old forms of resistance and added new ones. Yet the message is the same as GIs disengage from the wars.

This book examines the problems and questions that have led men and women in the military to resist the wars in Iraq and Afghanistan. It takes readers into the courtroom, where sailors, soldiers, and Marines have spoken out, arguing that these wars are illegal under international law, unconstitutional under U.S. law, and simply immoral. To date, argument and testimony have centered on Iraq, but that is changing as we begin to see soldiers resisting deployment to Afghanistan as well. Through the voices of service members and veterans, we explore those questions and the growing conviction among our troops that the wars are wrong. We then look at what service members and veterans have done—and what readers can do—to resist, and really end, these wars. As this book goes to press, the Bush administration and the Iraqi government have concluded a status of forces agreement. But it is not clear when and if President Obama will completely end the occupation of Iraq. And he has indicated his intention to expand the occupation of Afghanistan.

Rules of Disengagement is a practical guide, not an abstract analysis. Readers can use the examples of soldiers, veterans, and their families and the specific discussion of applicable regulations and laws to form their own conclusions and consider their own options. Whether soldiers, family members, friends, or simply concerned individuals, readers can use the material here to ponder the legal and moral questions soldiers are raising about the wars, and also to contemplate the effects of illegal warfare on the day-to-day conditions of soldiers' and their families' lives. Along the way, we can all reflect on ways to respond and, we hope, disengage.

ONE

Resisting Illegal Wars

LEGAL SCHOLARS HAVE ANALYZED the legality of the wars in Iraq and Afghanistan, and of Vietnam before them. But the legality of these wars is something that any soldier or civilian can consider—in plain language and with personal conclusions. Pablo Paredes, a young sailor confronted with these questions, and Howard Levy, an Army officer facing very similar issues during Vietnam, found themselves obliged to appraise the legality of these wars and their participation in them. Their analyses, and their examples of resistance, offer useful lessons for GIs today.

As you will see, military and federal courts in this country, much like their counterparts during the Vietnam War, have shown real resistance to reviewing the legality of these wars and of soldiers' orders to participate in them. Many judges have concluded that applying the law to the wars, and then to service members' refusal to take part in the wars, is not their role, not a matter under their jurisdiction, or not "relevant." But current cases also demonstrate that military judges, juries (called panels in courts-martial), and the public are increasingly sympathetic to these arguments, and to the fact that men and women of conscience have put their futures on the line for their opinions and actions against illegal wars and illegal orders. This sympathy has yet to show up in court-martial decisions about the law, but it often appears in lenient sentencing of resisters. Growing respect can be seen for those who have acted on strong and heartfelt opinions about duty and legal obligation. (Such leniency can also be seen, as described in the next chapter, in judges' sentencing of conscientious objectors who have refused orders.)

This chapter tells two stories, one old and one new, that offer insights into the process by which soldiers have concluded that they cannot participate in wars. It considers the application of the law of war to military law, as played out in individual cases and courts-martial.

Pablo Paredes and the Illegal War in Iraq

Petty Officer Third Class Pablo Paredes was born in Bronx, New York, the son of Ecuadoran and Puerto Rican immigrants. On December 6, 2004, Paredes refused orders to board the USS *Bonhomme Richard*, an amphibious assault ship scheduled to transport 3,000 Marines to Iraq. Paredes believed that the war in Iraq was illegal and that Marines who fought in Iraq were placed in a position to commit war crimes. By delivering the Marines to Iraq, Paredes felt he would be complicit as a war criminal. Paredes agonized about what he should do. He considered hurting himself, perhaps by breaking a bone—an arm or a leg—or asking a friend to do it for him. Or he could show up drunk or on drugs (even though he had never used drugs). He was desperate to avoid becoming part of the war machine. Finally, Paredes simply refused to go. The Navy charged him with unauthorized absence and missing his ship's movement by design.

Lt. Cdr. Robert Klant, the judge in Paredes' special court-martial, dismissed the unauthorized absence charge but convicted Paredes of missing movement by design. Before his sentencing,

Paredes told the judge, "In all I read, I came to an overwhelming conclusion supported by countless examples that any soldier who knowingly participates in an illegal war can find no haven in the fact that they were following orders, in the eyes of international law." He added, "I believe, as a member of the armed forces, beyond having a duty to my chain of command and my president, I have a higher duty to my conscience and to the supreme law of the land." Thus, he said, "Both of these higher duties dictate that I must not participate in any way, hands-on or indirect, in the current aggression that has been unleashed on Iraq."[1]

Judge Klant refused to allow expert testimony on the illegality of the war in the guilt phase of the court-martial. But he permitted one of the authors, Marjorie Cohn, to testify as an expert witness in the sentencing hearing. Cohn told the judge that the war in Iraq violates the United Nations Charter, which forbids a country from attacking another country unless it is acting in self-defense or with the approval of the Security Council:

> Since the invasion of Kuwait 11 to 12 years before Operation Iraqi Freedom, Iraq had not invaded any country and Iraq was not a threat to any country, including the United States. Iraq did not have weapons of mass destruction and that was clear; many weapons inspectors said that at the time. There was no link between 9/11 and Saddam Hussein's regime, or al-Qaeda and Saddam Hussein's regime. There was no imminent threat of any attack against the United States or any other member of the United Nations. And, therefore, it was not carried out in self-defense under Article 51 of the United Nations Charter.[2]

Furthermore, she said, the UN Security Council did not sanction the United States' use of force in Iraq. "In fact, just before the invasion of Iraq, the United States tried mightily to get the Security Council to pass a resolution authorizing the war. The

United States, Britain, and Spain tried to get a resolution through and were unable to."

Cohn explained that Paredes had a reasonable belief that transporting Marines to Iraq would make him complicit in the commission of war crimes. The U.S. War Crimes Act defines grave breaches of the Geneva Conventions as war crimes. Torture, inhumane treatment, willful killing, and the denial of a right to a fair trial constitute grave breaches.

The torture and abuse of prisoners at Abu Ghraib prison in Iraq by U.S. forces are war crimes, she said. "Beginning with the 'shock and awe,' the first dropping of 2,000 bombs on civilian areas constituted willful killing and a war crime under the Geneva Conventions. The forced deportation of 200,000 citizens of Fallujah and the retaliatory attack on Fallujah and destruction of a hospital also amounted to war crimes."

Both the Nuremberg Principles and the Uniform Code of Military Justice (UCMJ) establish a duty to obey lawful orders, but they also create a duty to disobey unlawful orders. In the UCMJ, Cohn told the judge, "it's not just the commission of war crimes, or crimes against the peace, or crimes against humanity that is punishable, but also complicity in the commission of those crimes."

"In criminal law," she noted, "we call it 'aiding and abetting.' So even if someone were not personally to go to Iraq and commit war crimes, if that person were transporting someone over to Iraq to commit war crimes, they would be liable for the war crimes just the same as the person who actually committed the war crimes."

Orders to board the ship and transport Marines to fight in an illegal war and possibly commit war crimes were unlawful. Paredes thus had a duty to refuse those unlawful orders to embark on the *Bonhomme Richard* on December 6, 2004.

At the conclusion of Cohn's testimony, Judge Klant, annoyed with an inept cross-examination by a Navy prosecutor, made a statement that astonished the spectators: "I believe the government has successfully demonstrated a reasonable belief for every service member to decide that the wars in Yugoslavia, Afghanistan and Iraq were illegal to fight in."[3]

The Navy prosecutor, Lt. B. T. Hale, asked the judge to sentence Paredes to nine months in the brig, forfeiture of pay and allowances, and a bad conduct discharge. The public nature of Paredes' protest made it more serious, the prosecutor argued. Paredes' civilian defense attorney from the National Lawyers Guild, Jeremy Warren, urged Judge Klant not to punish Paredes more harshly for exercising his right of free speech. Warren told the judge that Paredes refused to board the ship not, as many others had, for selfish reasons but rather as an act of conscience.

Judge Klant did not sentence Pablo Paredes to jail time or a bad conduct discharge for missing his ship's movement to the Persian Gulf. The judge gave Paredes two months' restriction to the base, three months' hard labor without confinement, and a reduction in rank to seaman recruit. Spectators on both sides of the aisle were stunned at the leniency of the sentence.

Howard Levy and the Illegal War in Vietnam

Forty years before Pablo Paredes refused to board his ship, the United States became embroiled in another illegal war. When the U.S. military began bombing North Vietnam in February 1965, the State Department argued that the infiltration of thousands of North Vietnamese into South Vietnam constituted an armed attack against a member of the United Nations, which allowed the United States to exercise collective self-defense under Article 51 of the UN Charter. An armed attack occurs only when substantial military forces cross an international boundary.

But South Vietnam was not a separate state or a member of the United Nations. Thus, the United States was not legally entitled to respond to a request for military assistance by South Vietnam. Moreover, according to the 1966 Mansfield Report, infiltration from the North before 1965 "was confined primarily to political cadres and military leadership."[4] The North introduced significant numbers of armed personnel into the South only after the United States had intervened militarily.

Like the American invasions of Iraq and Afghanistan, the U.S. military attack on North Vietnam violated the UN Charter. It was not executed in lawful self-defense, nor did the UN Security Council authorize the attack. Congress passed resolutions before the U.S. bombings of Vietnam, Iraq, and Afghanistan, purporting to authorize the use of military force in each case. These resolutions were based on misrepresentations by the U.S. government about the threats posed by North Vietnam and Saddam Hussein, respectively. Afghanistan did not mount an armed attack against the United States, and the Security Council did not sanction "Operation Enduring Freedom."[5]

The Johnson administration falsely claimed that a U.S. Navy destroyer had been attacked by North Vietnamese torpedo boats patrolling beyond territorial waters in August 1964; Congress responded with the now infamous Gulf of Tonkin Resolution. Likewise, the Bush administration hyped the existence of weapons of mass destruction in Iraq and ties between Hussein and al-Qaeda, knowing both claims to be false; Congress passed an authorization for the use of military force against Iraq in response.

Congress does not have the power to authorize a *crime against peace*, defined by the Nuremberg Charter as a war of aggression or one that violates international treaties. UN General Assembly Resolution 3314 (XXIX) defines *aggression* as the use of armed force by one state against the sovereignty, territorial integrity, or political independence of another state, or in any other manner inconsistent with the Charter of the United Nations. U.S. military force against both Vietnam and Iraq violated the UN Charter, an international treaty; both cases therefore constitute wars of aggressions, which are crimes against peace.

Resisters to the Vietnam War also argued that it was illegal. Dr. Howard Levy was a captain in the Army stationed at Fort Jackson, South Carolina, where he was assigned as chief of the Dermatological Service of the U.S. Army Hospital in July 1965. Levy opposed the war and thought black soldiers were being used as cannon fodder in that illegal conflict.

Levy disobeyed an order to train Special Forces or Green Beret aidmen (enlisted personnel with medical training attached to combat units) to be paramedics, saying it would violate his medical ethics. These aidmen would use their medical training to win the trust of the Vietnamese people, which would allow U.S. troops to move into the villages and carry out their military-political mission. In an interview in the 2005 film *Sir! No Sir!*, Levy said,

> I was asked to train Green Beret people, Special Forces men. Why were they training these guys in dermatology? Well they were training them to do dermatology in Vietnam because they knew that if they were able to offer a few simple remedies and help cure a few children of some simple bacterial infections that that would ingratiate themselves to the Vietnamese community. And you know, you remember the phrase *winning the hearts and minds of the people*; so this was how you were going to win the hearts and minds of the people, and while they were offering the Band-Aids of helping to cure a few cases of impetigo, they were bombing the hell out of the villages.

Levy objected to what he called the "prostitution of medicine," whereby medicine was converted into a weapon of war. "So it was a propaganda tool basically," Levy said. He felt these aidmen were committing war crimes. "Special Forces personnel are liars and thieves and killers of peasants and murderers of women and children."[6]

Levy's civil rights work—he helped register black voters in South Carolina—as well as his opposition to the war angered the Army. In 1967 Levy was charged at a general court-martial with willfully disobeying a lawful command of his superior commissioned officer, engaging in conduct unbecoming an officer and a gentleman, and publicly uttering certain statements to enlisted personnel with design to promote disloyalty and disaffection among the troops.

He now remembers being most impressed by the support he received from other GIs for the stand he had taken, when he saw the GI movement building. In *Sir! No Sir!,* Levy observed,

> I think the most startling thing to me occurred, however, as the court-martial began. What would happen was we would walk from the parking lot to the building where the court-martial was being held, and it was the most remarkable thing when hundreds, hundreds of GIs would hang out of windows, out of the barracks and give me the V-sign or give me the clenched fist. This was mind-boggling to me. This was a revelation, and at that point it really became crystal clear to me that something had changed here and that something very, very important was happening.

Levy tried to raise a Nuremberg defense, arguing that the war was illegal and immoral and that U.S. troops were committing war crimes in Vietnam. His witnesses testified about the mutilation of the dead; bounties put on enemies' heads, particularly the collection of ears as proof of killings; assassination; the use of weapons such as white phosphorous gas that cause unnecessary suffering; the forcible removal and relocation of civilians; wanton destruction of civilian property, including the burning of villages; and complicity in summary execution and torture, including waterboarding.

But the presiding judge ruled that "while there have been perhaps instances of needless brutality in this struggle in Vietnam about which the accused may have learned . . . there is no evidence that would render this order to train aidmen illegal on the grounds that eventually these men would become engaged in war crimes."[7] The court-martial was thus precluded from considering Levy's Nuremberg defense.

Levy told us that he wasn't surprised. "Even if you proved that some Green Beret people had committed war crimes, you still had to prove the ones I was training were going to do that. And that was a hard task to do. Everyone in Vietnam was committing war crimes . . . torching villages and throwing people out of planes and napalming children. It was the whole war. It wasn't just the Green Berets, although they were guilty too for sure. I can't imagine a military judge letting that go to a jury."

Levy was convicted of all three charges. The court-martial concluded that he "wrongfully and dishonorably" made "intemperate, defamatory, provoking, disloyal, contemptuous" statements that were "disrespectful" to Special Forces personnel and enlisted personnel who were patients or served under his supervision.

He was sentenced to dismissal from the service, the equivalent of a dishonorable discharge, forfeiture of all pay and allowances, and confinement for three years at hard labor. Levy spent nearly 26 months in the military stockade at Fort Leavenworth. The Supreme Court affirmed his convictions.

As these cases demonstrate, military courts are not enthusiastic about challenges to the legality of orders or the wars, or to their constitutional and international law underpinnings. What little testimony and argument about these issues have been used in the guilt phase of courts-martial have usually been presented as part of other arguments that challenge the intent and motivation elements of the charged offenses.

Although military judges are generally unwilling to grapple with international law and the constitutionality of military orders as a defense, or to admit that the military may have got it wrong on the law, a number have been sympathetic to these arguments as issues of mitigation in sentencing. As the Paredes case and others show, testimony about the legal basis of the war has helped courts understand that the accused may be grappling with real concerns about duty and honor and may not be acting out of expediency or cowardice. In some courtrooms resisters have been treated with a degree of respect, and sentences sometimes reflect this. But this approach can backfire. Soldiers arguing the illegality of the war as a defense risk receiving harsher treatment—certainly military courts have been more lenient toward quiet soldiers with family or medical problems than toward those speaking out publicly from personal beliefs.

The response Pablo Paredes and other resisters have received from fellow soldiers, and public respect for their positions, undoubtedly played a role in legitimizing the validity of their beliefs, if not the arguments themselves. Like civilian courts, military courts-martial are influenced indirectly by popular opinion about the legality of the wars and the courage of resisters. And the illegality of the wars has had a significant effect in the courts of public opinion. Not constrained by the military's narrow view of legal issues, people in the United States and the rest of the world consider these important questions, particularly when they are articulated by the men and women ordered to carry out illegal wars and occupation.

· TWO ·

Modern Conscientious Objectors

SOLDIERS INVARIABLY CONSIDER the morality of the wars in which they participate and the means by which those wars are carried out. American GIs face very personal questions about the right or wrong of the wars in Iraq and Afghanistan, their roles in those wars, and the methods of warfare—the rules of engagement. For many, of course, the answers depend on the specifics. World War II was different in many fundamental ways from the war in Vietnam. But military law and regulations allow soldiers to disengage and seek noncombatant status or discharge only if they have religious, moral, or ethical objection to all war, or, in the language of the regulations, "war in any form."

This chapter offers a brief definition of conscientious objection, then discusses several conscientious objectors, including some whose beliefs do not fit the military's limited terms. Their own statements and stories reveal the legal process and the practical experience involved in applying for CO status. Perhaps more than with any other type of discharge or dissent, the legal terms for modern COs were established by cases during the Vietnam War. And we discuss the substantive rights they won before moving on to the current regulations and the process of applying for discharge or noncombatant status as a CO.

Conscientious objection has a long and honorable history in the American military, with cases going back to the colonies and the Revolutionary War. Through litigation and public pressure, COs have expanded the definition of conscientious objection and the rights of CO applicants over the years, forcing the military to recognize a wide range of religious and moral beliefs as a basis for objection and to treat objectors with some measure of respect and dignity. Soldiers and sailors like those discussed in this chapter have demanded that the military obey the courts and its own regulations. These objectors' efforts have helped to protect and expand GIs' rights in other discharges and dissent as well.

Defining a Conscientious Objector

Our law has a well-established procedure for becoming a conscientious objector. The Supreme Court in *United States v. Seeger* quoted Chief Justice Hughes, who said that "in the forum of conscience, duty to a moral power higher than the State has always been maintained."[1]

Under Department of Defense and service regulations, the military must grant CO status to any service member who is conscientiously opposed to participation in war in any form, whose opposition is founded on religious training and beliefs, and whose position is sincere and deeply held.[2] Religious or moral objection to participation in war must have developed or become central to the CO's beliefs after entry into the military. Although this requirement is not stated in the regulations, the military assumes that the objection grows out of a fundamental belief that it is wrong to take human life through military force.

"Religious training and belief" is broadly defined to include "deeply held moral or ethical belief, to which all else is subordinate or upon which all else is ultimately dependent, and which has the power or force to affect moral well-being." It cannot be merely "a belief which rests solely upon considerations of policy, pragmatism, expediency or political views." Relevant factors to be considered include "training in the home and church; general demeanor and pattern of conduct; participation in religious activities; whether ethical or moral convictions were gained through training, study, contemplation, or other activity comparable in rigor and dedication to the processes by which traditional religious convictions are formulated; credibility of the applicant; and credibility of persons supporting the claim." "Sincerity" is determined by an impartial evaluation of the applicant's thinking and living in its totality, past and present.[3]

"War in any form" means all wars rather than a specific war. The applicant has the burden of proving by clear and convincing evidence that he or she is a CO. An applicant who would have qualified for CO status before entering the military is generally not eligible to be a CO once in the service. A military decision to deny an application for CO status will be overturned by a court only if no factual basis exists for the decision.

Camilo Mejía: "Prisoner of Conscience"

Camilo Mejía was the first publicly known conscientious objector to the Iraq war. The son of famed Nicaraguan Sandinista troubadour Carlos Mejía Godoy, Mejía joined the U.S. Army because it offered him health care, financial stability, the possibility of going to college, and, most of all, camaraderie, friends, and community.

In April 2003, eight years after he entered the Florida National Guard, Staff Sgt. Mejía was sent to Iraq. One day he went on a search-and-destroy mission. He saw the body of a large man on the side of the road, covered with what looked like a white sheet.

A small child stood beside the corpse of his father. "I subsequently tried to remember the boy's face, whether he was crying or looked sad, but the more I tried to remember the more I realized that there are moments my memory will just never let me revisit," Mejía wrote in his book, *Road from Ar Ramadi*. Mejía spoke of the evils of war. "The truth as I see it now is that in a war, the bad is often measured against what's even worse, and that, in turn, makes a lot of deplorable things seem permissible. When that happens, the imaginary line between right and wrong starts to vanish in a heavy fog, until it disappears completely and decisions are weighed on a scale of values that is profoundly corrupt."[4]

While he was in Iraq, Mejía's faith led him to oppose all war. "Prior to going to Iraq, I had never really prayed and my faith had mostly stayed on the surface," he noted. As time went on, Mejía began to pray for the soldiers in his unit, then for all the soldiers in Iraq and their families. "Before long I was praying for the families of the Iraqis we killed during our missions. And then one day I realized I was even praying for our enemies, and for an end to violence in Iraq, and then for an end to all war."[5]

After serving in the infantry in Iraq for five months, Mejía came home on leave. He struggled mightily with conflicting urges—to return to Iraq and be with his men or to remain and refuse to kill or be killed. Mejía went back and forth in his mind.

> If I returned to the war, I could be killed in more than one way. It wasn't just the physical death; it was also the many deaths of the soul every time you kill a human being. Whether we squeeze the trigger, give the order, or simply stand idle in the face of senseless missions that result in the spilling of innocent blood, it doesn't make a difference. We die, little by little, each time someone gets killed, until there is no soul left, and the body becomes a corpse, breathing and warm but devoid of humanity.[6]

Mejía didn't board the plane to return to Iraq. But he knew the war would not be over for him. It would be a war "to reclaim my humanity and my spiritual freedom." It would be "a war against the system I had come from, a battle against the military machine, the imperial dragon that devours its own soldiers and Iraqi civilians alike for the sake of profits." Henceforth, Mejía would fight only with his words. "I knew that somehow I had to turn my words into weapons, that speaking out was now my only way to fight."[7] He would later write, "I realize now that my refusal to participate in a morally indefensible war was one I should have made from the beginning. But it took the experience of going to war for me to see things in a broader perspective and realize that I was, deep down, a conscientious objector."[8]

And speak out he did. In media interviews, Mejía opposed the war. He went underground and immediately had a support system, which included attorney Louis Font, himself a resister during the Vietnam War. Font had faced 25 years in prison, and his trial proceedings lasted a year. He was eventually declared a conscientious objector and released with an honorable discharge.

Mejía spent countless hours filling out his CO application. On March 15, 2004, five months after he refused to go back to Iraq, Mejía surrendered to the authorities after making a public statement in which he declared himself to be a conscientious objector. "So if you want to support troops," he said, "you cannot support the war."[9]

The Army charged Mejía with desertion: quitting his unit with intent to avoid hazardous duty. At his court-martial, Mejía challenged the legality of the war and the conduct of U.S. troops toward Iraqi civilians. But the judge ruled that the jury would not hear Mejía's evidence on the illegality of the war, war crimes, or crimes against humanity during the guilt phase of the trial. Mejía was convicted of desertion with intent to avoid hazardous duty.

Francis Boyle, a professor at the Illinois College of Law, testified during the sentencing phase that Mejía could not be charged with desertion for refusing an order to fight in an illegal war: "Under the Laws of War Sergeant Mejía had the right, if not the obligation, to abstain from any participation in the commission of war crimes, let alone doing it himself or turning people, prisoners, over, where they would be subject to abuse."[10] Former attorney general Ramsey Clark testified that "the word 'quit' is defined in Article 85 as a person who leaves or fails to return without authority. His authority is the Nuremberg Charter. It's The Hague and Geneva Conventions."[11]

Mejía was sentenced to 12 months confinement, reduction in rank to E-1, one year's forfeiture of pay, and a bad conduct discharge. Mejía wrote that as he walked down the steps to the police car, "that was the moment that I gained my freedom. I understood then that freedom is not something physical, but a condition of the mind and of the heart. On that day I learned that there is no greater freedom than the freedom to follow one's conscience. That day I was free, in a way I had never been before."[12]

Camilo Mejía was named the Iraq war's first "prisoner of conscience" by Amnesty International. He served nine months in prison. In August 2007 Mejía was elected chairman of the board of directors of Iraq Veterans Against the War. As this book goes to press, his conscientious objection petition is still pending.

Conscientious Objection Today

Hundreds of GIs have filed CO applications, while many more service members with CO beliefs have sought discharge in other ways, gone absent without leave (AWOL), or refused orders to deploy to combat zones. The conscientious objectors profiled in this chapter are just a small number of the many service members who have applied for CO status since 9/11.

The Army tried to deploy Sergeant Corey Martin to Afghanistan in 2006 while his CO application was still pending, but the New York Civil Liberties Union sued in federal district court on his behalf and obtained an injunction preventing the deployment. The Army investigating officer who reviewed Martin's application during the first stage of the three-step CO discharge process recommended that his application be approved. The officer determined that Martin "is sincere in his beliefs of conscientious objection ... with the underlying belief as his opposition to all wars and the intentional consequence which war produces, which is casualties and suffering it produces to innocent civilians."[13] The Army relented and granted Martin CO status and an honorable discharge.

Several GIs whose CO applications were denied later petitioned successfully for habeas corpus relief—a legal procedure in which a judge can rule that person is being unlawfully held—and were granted CO status in federal court.

Dr. Mary Hanna's habeas petition was approved by the U.S. District Court for the District of Massachusetts in October 2006. Here's what happened: Hanna, an anesthesiologist, joined the Army in 1997 and filed for CO status in December 2005. Raised as an active member of the Coptic Orthodox Church, Hanna questioned her faith during college, but the turning point for her came in 2003 when her father died and she finally felt free to explore the contradiction between her religious beliefs and the Army mission. "Christ teaches unconditional love for both friend and enemy," she wrote. Hanna, who noted that Jesus Christ was a pacifist, said, "I believe that I betray these moral and religious principles by participating in war in any way." The district court found no basis in fact for the Army's conclusion that Hanna failed to qualify for CO status.[14]

The Army appealed the district court's ruling to the court of appeals. To date, Hanna's case is the only one in which the military has appealed a district court opinion granting CO status. The appellate court, in a 2–1 ruling, affirmed the decision of the district court, finding that the Army's decision had no basis in fact.[15] The court of appeals stated that to prevail, the government would have had to show "some hard, reliable, provable facts which would provide a basis for disbelieving the applicant's sincerity" or "something concrete in the record which substantially blurs the picture painted by the applicant." The Army's reasons for its decision "must be grounded in logic," and "a mere suspicion is an inadequate basis in fact." The court went on to reject the Army's arguments that the timing of Hanna's application cast doubt on her sincerity and that her explanations for the change in her beliefs were inconsistent.

In January 2007 the U.S. District Court for the Southern District of California granted James Janke's habeas corpus petition. Janke submitted a request for discharge from the Marines in November 2004, stating that his moral and ethical beliefs led him to oppose participation in war. After completing a series of interviews and getting positive recommendations at every level, Janke's request was disapproved by the commandant of the Marine Corps. San Diego federal court judge Napoleon Jones concluded that the commandant had no basis in fact for denying Janke's request.[16] Janke had enlisted in the Marine Corps Reserves in February 2001. After his father's death in 2003, Janke began to rethink his most basic values and reconnected with his Catholic faith. As a result, he came to believe that participation in war is morally wrong. In July 2004 Janke contacted Larry Christian of the San Diego Military Counseling Project, who informed him that his beliefs qualified for discharge as a conscientious objector and provided him with information regarding criteria and procedures for requesting a discharge. Christian characterized the district court decision as "especially important for two reasons. First, because the Marine Corps has routinely denied discharge to conscientious objectors for spurious reasons, and now there is a court decision saying they cannot continue to do so without challenge. The second is that, to my knowledge, this is the first habeas corpus petition for a Marine conscientious objector granted during the present [Iraq] war. It's a sign that the tide is turning and that opposition to war from inside the military is gaining legitimacy in the public eye."[17]

Three months after Janke's victory in federal court, Robert Zabala's habeas corpus petition was granted by the U.S. District Court for the Northern District of California, and he was discharged from the Marines. In this case Zabala signed up for eight years in the Marines Corps Reserves under the Delayed Entry Program in July 2002. His beliefs changed dramatically after the death of his grandmother and his own brutalization in boot camp. When he heard his commander talk of "blowing shit up" and "kicking some fucking ass," Zabala wondered "how someone could be so motivated to kill." He said, "I realized that I was different than the rest of the men around me, that I had a different perspective and value of life than others." Zabala "began to think about the thousands of people who died in the past year in war, who didn't die due to just one soldier or suicide bomber, but largely by an organization. This organization trains to kill human life. This organization places mission accomplishment above human life... Every part of the Marine Corps, be it Radio Operator to Food Preparation, participates to keep this organization moving along on its mission to end human life."[18]

Dr. Timothy Watson, a captain in the Army's Individual Ready Reserve, prevailed in his habeas petition to the U.S. District Court for the Eastern District of New York in April 2007.[19] This is how it happened: Watson's opposition to the wars in Afghanistan and Iraq ultimately evolved into an opposition to all war. "As a form of retaliation and under the pretense of national security," Watson wrote, "the United States military has invaded and occupied a foreign country in an unprecedented preemptive war and I have become a doctor who now views war as an unacceptable lapse of reason, the ultimate act of futility and an entirely shameful human endeavor." Watson characterized caring for the injured so they could return to fight as the "weaponizing of human beings." He wrote, "In the Army, my work to heal would result, however indirectly, in the infliction of unnecessary wounds and loss of life."[20]

When Specialist Augustín Aguayo joined the Army in January 2003, he was not an objector. But in training Aguayo had difficulty firing at human-shaped silhouettes and stabbing human mannequins. "I felt guilty when I had to pick up and hold a weapon and practice killing with it," he recalled. After his tour as a medic in Iraq, he submitted a CO application. While the application was being processed, Aguayo was sent back to Iraq, where he was decorated for his service even though he refused to load his gun. Instead of being treated as a noncombatant, he was given guard duty and placed in dangerous positions with an unloaded weapon.

In his application Aguayo wrote, "My moral view does not allow me to take the life of another human being ... I believe that violence of any kind, or supporting thereof, for example being a combat medic (assisting the injured to later go back to a combat area) is not acceptable. My conscience will not allow me to continue down this path."[21]

Despite favorable recommendations, Aguayo's CO application was denied by the Secretary of the Army. He took his case to the U.S. District Court for the District of Columbia, which has jurisdiction over court cases concerning U.S. military personnel stationed abroad. The district court upheld the Pentagon's decision. Aguayo appealed the denial of his petition to the Court of Appeals for the District of Columbia Circuit. There, a three-judge panel sided with the Army, and the full court of appeals denied a petition for further review. Meanwhile, Aguayo's unit was slated to deploy to Iraq for the second time. He went AWOL, missed deployment, and turned himself in the next day. When the Army told him he had to go to Iraq, handcuffed and shackled if necessary, he fled his base in Germany and surrendered again in the United States several weeks later.

He was charged with desertion to avoid hazardous duty and missing movement by design, and tried by general court-martial in Wuerzburg, Germany, in March 2007. Because the courtroom was filled to overflowing, the judge authorized a closed-circuit video feed into a separate room. Aguayo pleaded guilty to lesser charges, and while he faced confinement for two and one-half years and a dishonorable discharge, he received a relatively lenient sentence: eight months confinement, with credit for 161 days of pretrial confinement; a bad conduct discharge; and a reduction in rank and forfeitures of pay.[22]

Aguayo filed a petition for writ of certiorari in the U.S. Supreme Court, asking the Court to review his case. The petition was denied in March 2008.

The first female GI to publicly take a stand against the Iraq war and to declare herself a conscientious objector was Specialist Katherine Jashinski of the Texas Army National Guard. Jashinski had enlisted in the guard as a cook in April 2002 at the age of 19. Although she believed that killing was wrong, she considered war an exception to that rule. But two years later, when she received activation orders to deploy to Afghanistan, she was forced to reevaluate her beliefs. Jashinski requested discharge based on conscientious objection, saying in a public statement, "Because I believe so strongly in nonviolence, I cannot perform any role in the military. Any person doing any job in the Army contributes in some way to the planning, preparation or implementation of war."[23] The Army denied her application, claiming she had presented little evidence of CO status. Jashinski, too, went to district court, which upheld the Army's decision. J. E. McNeil, from the Center on Conscience and War and one of Jashinski's attorneys, said, "Denying Katherine CO status is yet another in a long line of actions by the military to defy its own rules in order to get the numbers of soldiers they need to continue this war."[24]

Jashinski was court-martialed for refusing to train with weapons. She pleaded guilty to the charge of refusal to obey a legal order. But the court-martial acquitted her of the more serious charge of missing movement by design. Jashinski told the military judge, "I'm a conscientious objector and I'm morally opposed to using weapons for any reason, including training." Testimony had been given about the sincerity of her opposition to all war. Although the judge did not find Jashinski's CO claim relevant to her guilt, he agreed that it could be considered in extenuation and mitigation during the sentencing phase. Jashinski received a bad conduct discharge and was sentenced to 120 days confinement.[25]

Aidan Delgado is a Buddhist who received conscientious objector status after spending nine months in Iraq. Here's how it happened: Delgado worked in the battalion headquarters at the Abu Ghraib prison. After his discharge, he set down his thoughts and experiences, which were published in a book, *The Sutras of Abu Ghraib: Notes from a Conscientious Objector in Iraq*. Confirming the International Committee of the Red Cross' conclusion that 70 to 90 percent of the prisoners were in the prison by mistake,

Delgado said that most prisoners were suspected only of petty theft, public drunkenness, forging documents, and impersonating officials. "At Abu Ghraib, we shot prisoners for protesting their conditions; four were killed," Delgado maintained, calling Abu Ghraib "a leviathan of oppression, negligence, and monstrous cruelty."[26] Delgado told a San Diego audience that he has photographs of troops "scooping their [prisoners'] brains out."

In the summer of 2003, two years after Delgado enlisted in the Army Reserve, he wrote, "I feel intensely hypocritical, believing in compassion, mediation, and nonviolence while simultaneously carrying a machine gun and serving in an occupation force. The conflict seems irreconcilable. Every day that I stay in the military I feel more a traitor to my beliefs . . . I've come to see the Army in its worst form, a distortion of itself: violence, threats, dogma, and hatred. I see the way the soldiers bully each other for dominance, and then watch as those who are bullied turn and dominate the Iraqis."[27]

After the funeral of Specialist Eric Ramirez, a fellow soldier who was killed by an improvised explosive device (IED) in Iraq, Delgado wrote

> *Do not take life.* It's written in the powdered bones of the grave pit in Nasiriyah. It's written in the wet, pink brains of prisoners shot down at Abu Ghraib. It's written in the razor wire and the rotting food. It's written in the eyes of the soldiers who've turned, their hearts gone black. It's written on the lips of all those who smile to hear of another's cruelty. It's written in all the blank stares of the innocent men caged like animals. It's written in that empty helmet and pair of boots that once held a human soul. At long last, after twenty-two years of life and a year of war, it's written broad and clear across my heart.[28]

Delgado filed for CO status while still stationed in Iraq. Despite continued mortar bombardment of Abu Ghraib at the time, his command took away his ballistic plates (ceramic shields fitted into a flak vest to protect against high-velocity bullets), which are essential for survival in a combat zone. Delgado was physically attacked by other soldiers, but, like other COs who believe in the use of nonlethal force, he turned the tables, taking one assailant down in a wrestling hold. In his CO interview with an investigating officer, Delgado explained that while Buddhism taught him to turn the other cheek, it didn't mean he was a doormat. The officer recommended that Delgado's CO application be granted, and the Army affirmed that decision.

The Department of Defense claims that COs are few in numbers and that support for the war is high among military personnel. The Government Accountability Office (GAO) reported in 2007 that 425 service members had filed CO applications between 2002 and 2006.[29] In its report the GAO acknowledged that its figures included only applications that were reported to service headquarters by local commands. GAO noted that its researchers "found limitations with the consistency and completeness of the data that could result in a possible understatement of the number of applications," but the agency decided that the information was sufficiently reliable to show trends.[30] Attorneys and military counseling groups working with conscientious objectors say that these figures are in fact extremely low, the likely result of intentional understatement by the DoD. The data also do not include soldiers and sailors discharged for other reasons, or those who went AWOL or refused orders and were subsequently discharged administratively or as the result of courts-martial. Nor do they include the many service members whose CO applications were "denied" by sergeants, chiefs, or officers who refused to forward the applications as required by the regulations, a problem widely reported by CO applicants.

The realities of military life and combat in Iraq and Afghanistan lead many soldiers to question the legitimacy of the wars. A good number of these soldiers come to the conclusion, on the basis of religious, moral, or ethical beliefs that developed since enlistment, that all war is wrong. Some serve in spite of those beliefs, feeling bound by their military contracts and seldom knowing that conscientious objection is sanctioned in military regulations and protected by law. In fact, a large number of service members with CO beliefs remain in the service or go AWOL under the misapprehension that they do not qualify for CO status.

Conscientious Objection during Vietnam

Although all of this nation's wars have had their CO resisters, the Department of Defense did not create formal CO regulations until 1962. The first regulations narrowly defined conscientious objection to exclude all those without traditional religious CO beliefs.

Military and draft objectors during the Vietnam War greatly expanded the law of conscientious objection, while a shift in public opinion about the war (encouraged by the GI antiwar movement) influenced judicial decisions. Cases like *United States v. Seeger* and *Welsch v. United States* paved the way for CO status for those whose objection was not based on traditional religious beliefs; included were those for whom moral or ethical beliefs took the place of traditional religious beliefs.[31]

Other objectors from Vietnam to the present have challenged the military's assumption that COs must object to all violence. Draft cases going back to the 1950s held that COs may believe in personal self-defense and that use of force to restrain another from violence as a last resort is not inconsistent with CO beliefs. Muhammad Ali, then known as Cassius Clay, helped win court and public recognition that COs need not be total pacifists. Although military decisions usually acknowledge this notion, it has never been added to the regulations.

Despite the stereotypes, COs come from a wide range of social, economic, and racial backgrounds. Soldiers who were turned down because they lacked religious sophistication or because they spoke or wrote poorly challenged the military's assumption that COs must be articulate, erudite, and sophisticated. Reviewing officers and military headquarters frequently denied claims because applicants did not show theological scholarship or speak like college students. In the *Seeger* case, the Supreme Court noted that in CO cases "one deals with the beliefs of different individuals who will articulate them in a multitude of ways."[32] COs since then have used the courts to demand that their beliefs need not be set forth at length or eloquently, causing one court to state, "we believe, nevertheless, that not only the articulate may qualify as conscientious objectors."[33]

Over the years many applicants have been turned down because they held political beliefs about specific wars or U.S. foreign policy. In many cases political beliefs and actions were based entirely on underlying moral or religious beliefs that warranted CO status; in some, political beliefs existed side by side with deeply held spiritual beliefs. Many of these soldiers were denied CO status because the military claimed that their political beliefs were inconsistent with or more important than their religious or moral beliefs. A number of applicants took their cases to court, where federal judges agreed that opposition to a specific war is not inconsistent with belief against all wars and held that qualifying objection to war could rest on political as well as religious reasons.

Nevertheless, the services continue to view objectors more harshly if they express political views or act on them. The Navy concluded that when Pablo Paredes applied to be a CO, he was motivated by political rather than moral objection, using this as a reason to deny his claim. Nonetheless, soldiers with political views still succeed in establishing CO status.

Although the military continues to make the process difficult, the efforts of objectors during the Vietnam era, and since then, have greatly expanded the definition of conscientious objection.

Applying for CO Status Today: Myths, Regulations, and Resources

The military offers its members little information about conscientious objection or other discharges, and most soldiers never see the regulations that govern them. But military culture contains a number of odd myths and stereotypes about conscientious objection. Objectors are commonly portrayed as extremely religious, idealistic, and somewhat naive soldiers who come from traditional "peace churches," who wear their religious beliefs on their sleeves, and who are likely to pray in public and read the Bible or scholarly moral texts in the barracks. Objectors, it is thought, will always turn the other cheek, because they are total and lifelong pacifists who would no more raise their voices to a sergeant than they would hurt a fly.

The myths about COs also portray them as intellectuals, fluent in Bible studies, well-read, well-spoken, and soft-spoken. COs are considered to be white upper-class college students who stumbled into the military by accident. And despite common social beliefs about the gentle nature of women, COs are commonly assumed to be men.

During the Vietnam War, COs were viewed as subversives and cowards, though after the war many came to see them as honorable

40

soldiers following their conscience. The current military stereotype harkens back to Vietnam: COs are afraid of the dangers of combat and are taking the easy way out, probably lying about their beliefs. As public protests increase, so does the attitude that COs are motivated by political opinions rather than moral or religious beliefs. Of course, soldiers serving in peacetime often hear that they can apply for CO status only if there is a war, but those serving during wartime hear that applying is useless because all applications will be denied until the war is over. Finally, the story they hear says that to be discharged as a CO is almost impossible, that the process will take at least two years, that the discharge will be other than honorable, and that COs cannot receive federal benefits or get federal jobs.

Needless to say, these myths are not true. The examples in this chapter show that COs are real people with a wide variety of beliefs who have acted on the mandates of their conscience.

Fortunately, service members and their families can find a great deal of accurate and useful data by looking outside the military. The resources and organizations described in this chapter provide a wealth of information about the criteria for CO status and procedures for applications, and they offer much legal and moral support for those who apply.

Information about conscientious objection is available from a number of civilian organizations. The national GI Rights Network (at www.girightshotline.org and 877-447-4487), organizations like the National Lawyers Guild's Military Law Task Force (at www.nlgmltf.org and 619-463-2369), the Center on Conscience and War (at www.centeronconscience.org and 800-379-2679), and a number of other military counseling groups provide information, regulations, and assistance to CO applicants and other soldiers. The applicable regulations, available on these civilian Web sites, contain important information. But the CO process is complex, and the regulations contain some pitfalls. Service members who wish to apply for CO status are well advised to seek help from counseling organizations or civilian lawyers experienced in military law when preparing and submitting their applications.

COs must answer a number of questions on their applications. The most important of these questions ask for detailed information in essay form about an applicant's basic beliefs, history, and lifestyle; beliefs about the use of force and violence; and the effects the person's beliefs have had on his or her life. With the application COs should submit letters of support—a must according to counselors and attorneys—from family members, friends, priests or ministers, fellow soldiers, or others who can attest to the CO's sincerity. Military reviewers often go through applications and letters with a fine-tooth comb. Thus, the applicant and attorney or counselor should spend time drafting and reviewing the application to ensure that it is clear and does not unintentionally deviate from the official criteria.

Applicants for CO status must be interviewed by a military psychiatrist, or another medical officer if a psychiatrist is not available; a chaplain; and an investigating officer (IO). The IO reviews the application before interviewing the applicant and sometimes conducts an investigation by questioning other soldiers and examining the applicant's record and outside statements. The psychiatrist attests to the CO's good mental health; the chaplain and investigating officer offer opinions about the CO's beliefs, and the IO makes a recommendation for acceptance or denial of the CO claim.

Regulations specifically suggest that reviewers look for ulterior motives—other reasons such as pending deployments, medical or family problems, or attractive civilian employment opportunities—that might be the real impetus for the CO application. The stereotypes and myths about objectors can cause serious problems, as the psychiatrist (despite his or her neutral role), chaplain, and investigating officer are often swayed by those biases. Their reports frequently show that they judge an applicant's beliefs and sincerity on the basis of their own ideas about what the CO should believe, rather than the requirements of the regulations. Because of this, some COs bring an attorney or military counselor to the IO's interview, make a recording of it, or both.

CO applicants and counsel may rebut these recommendations, as well as subsequent recommendations prepared by their commanding officers. Unless commands are sloppy or duplicitous, the entire application, with reports, rebuttals if any, and recommendations, is submitted to military headquarters, where an official or a review board makes a final determination on the claim. Those whose claims are wrongly denied may take their cases to federal court.

While their applications are pending, COs may face difficult questions about performing military duties that conflict directly with their beliefs. The regulations vary slightly, but all suggest that commands assign applicants duties that are least inconsistent with their beliefs. By law COs may refuse to bear arms or use them, but they have no similar right to refuse other duties. Soldiers may refuse to load or shoot a weapon, but they may not refuse to go on patrol. Soldiers may be forced to deploy to a combat zone, but they are not required to engage in combat there. In fact, unfriendly commands sometimes deny protective gear and armor to COs in combat areas as a form of retaliation; for example, Aidan Delgado was subjected to this treatment.

For a number of COs, the conflict between duties and CO beliefs is too great to accept—refusals to deploy to Iraq or Afghanistan, or to use weapons there, have framed a number of CO cases in the past few years, including some of those detailed in this chapter.

The CO process is one of the most legally protected of discharge proceedings—COs have greater rights than those who seek discharge for family hardship or similar reasons (see Chapter 8). But command hostility to COs often results in refusals to grant them the rights available under the regulations, so that some applicants must choose between obeying and refusing illegal orders. Their CO claims are postponed while they challenge the orders in courts-martial or civilian court. Fortunately, familiarity with the regulations and use of outside legal support often smooth the process. Some commands, and many fellow soldiers, recognize the courage that COs show in standing against military tradition and political expediency, so that despite the reports of problems and reprisals, many COs are discharged or assigned to noncombatant duties without serious problems.

Success rates vary among the services and, as noted above, some CO applications never reach military headquarters, as COs are discharged for other reasons or compelled to go AWOL or refuse orders. Although more CO applications have been denied in the past few years than in the decade before, many succeed without the necessity of court intervention.

Readers interested in the religious and moral issues involved in conscientious objection can find useful material through the civilian counseling organizations. The Central Committee for Conscientious Objectors' *Advice for Conscientious Objectors in the Armed Forces* offers a detailed discussion of various CO beliefs and CO procedures, and the Center on Conscience and War's *Words of Conscience* includes brief statements on conscientious objection from Christian, Jewish, Islamic, Hindu, Baha'i, Buddhist, and other faiths, as well as from moral and spiritual leaders such as Mahatma Gandhi, Henry David Thoreau, and Dr. Martin Luther King Jr. Thoughtful discussions of CO beliefs are available on the Web sites of the GI Rights Network and other groups.[34]

Although the CO process has allowed many soldiers a legal way to disengage from the wars, the realities of our moral beliefs do not always fit neatly into little legal boxes. For many, asserting their religious or ethical opposition to one or both of the current wars has meant refusal of orders or going AWOL, risking court-martial. For other objectors, disengagement means dissenting within the military, in any of a wide variety of ways discussed in Chapter 4.

· THREE ·

Winter Soldier

These are the times that try men's souls. The
summer soldier and the sunshine patriot will,
in this crisis, shrink from the service of their
country; but he that stands by it now deserves
the love and thanks of man and woman.

—THOMAS PAINE, 1776

THE BEST WAY TO UNDERSTAND the rules of engagement, and
to consider their misuse and violation, is to hear the stories told by
veterans of the wars in Iraq and Afghanistan. Embedded journalists are shielded from the reality, and legal scholars consider the
rules primarily in the abstract. But the GIs who have been there
tell chilling stories of ever-shifting rules that bear little relation
to the norms of international law or human rights. This chapter
begins with a brief history of the first Winter Soldier Investigation,
which was called by Vietnam Veterans Against the War in 1971 to
tell the American people about war crimes beyond imagination.
The testimony of soldiers who have served in Iraq and Afghanistan
reveals that the military has not learned the sobering lessons of the
Vietnam War, and that war crimes today are frighteningly similar to those committed 40 years ago. We discuss no regulations
here—the legal violations are set out in Chapter 1, and the rules of
dissent protecting and sometimes limiting such testimony follow

45

in Chapter 4. Here we consider just the unvarnished truth about the wars our government has authorized in our names.

Winter Soldier 1971

In 1969 Seymour Hersh broke the story of the 1968 My Lai Massacre, in which U.S. soldiers had killed up to 500 unarmed old men, women, and children during the Vietnam War. The shock waves from the revelation reverberated across the United States and around the world. Other stories of the torture, rape, and murder of Vietnamese civilians at the hands of the Americans emerged.

Vietnam Veterans Against the War joined forces with labor, religious, and celebrity activists to produce the Winter Soldier Investigation. The name was designed to contrast with Thomas Paine's famous words—the "summer soldier and the sunshine patriot" who shrank from the service of their country. Paine was speaking about those who deserted at Valley Forge because the going got rough. "Like the winter soldiers of 1776 who stayed after they had served their time, we veterans of Vietnam know that America is in grave danger," William Crandell from the First Marine Division said in his opening statement at the Winter Soldier hearings.[1]

During three days in late January and early February of 1971, in Detroit, Michigan, more than 100 veterans gave testimony documenting atrocities that they and others had committed in Vietnam. Most of those who testified had served on the front lines in the infantry. Their stories were emotional, gripping, and powerful. Yet the media largely ignored the event, and the scant coverage it did receive was hostile.

Crandell explained, "What threatens our country is not Redcoats or even Reds; it is our crimes that are destroying our national unity by separating those of our countrymen who deplore these acts from those of our countrymen who refuse to examine what is being done in America's name ... We are here to bear witness not against America, but against those policy makers who are perverting America."

Capt. Rusty Sachs, a helicopter pilot from August 1966 to September 1967, testified about the leveling of villages "for no valid reason, [and] throwing Viet Cong suspects from the aircraft after binding and gagging them with copper wire." Sachs said they had no instruction in the Geneva Conventions and were never told how to treat prisoners. Indeed, another witness, David Bishop, reported, "Usually we didn't have any prisoners. The prisoners were exterminated."[2]

Sgt. Scott Camile, a forward observer in Vietnam, recounted the "burning of villages with civilians in them, cutting off of ears, cutting off of heads, torturing of prisoners, calling in of artillery on villages for games, corpsmen killing wounded prisoners, napalm dropped on villages, women being raped, women and children being massacred, CS gas used on people, animals slaughtered, ... bodies shoved out of helicopters, tear-gassing people for fun and running civilian vehicles off the road." Camile said, "They usually drop two big canisters of napalm at a time. It just burns everything up, including the people."[3]

Fred Nienke joined the Marines Corps right out of high school in 1966. He testified about the effects of white phosphorus (known as "Willie Peter"). "It's probably one of the worst sights I've ever seen, is a person that's been burned by Willie Peter, because it doesn't stop. It just burns all completely through your body."[4]

Joe Bangert went to Vietnam in 1968. His testimony covered "the slaughter of civilians, the skinning of a Vietnamese woman, ... and the crucifixion of Vietnamese, either suspects or civilians."[5]

Twenty-seven-year-old Navy Lieutenant John Kerry attended the Winter Soldier Investigation. Three months later, Kerry testified before the Senate Foreign Relations Committee in a packed hearing room lined with television cameras. Kerry described the investigation to the senators. "Over 150 honorably discharged, and many very highly decorated, veterans testified to war crimes committed in Southeast Asia." Kerry continued:

> It is impossible to describe to you exactly what did happen in Detroit—the emotions in the room, and the feelings of the men who were reliving their experiences in Vietnam. They relived the absolute horror of what this country, in a sense, made them do. They told stories that at times they had personally raped, cut off ears, cut off heads, taped wires from portable telephones to human genitals and turned up the power, cut off limbs, blown up bodies, randomly shot at civilians, razed villages in fashion reminiscent of Genghis Khan, shot cattle and dogs for fun, poisoned food stocks, and generally ravaged the countryside of South Vietnam in addition to the normal ravage of war and the normal and very particular ravaging which is done by the applied bombing power of this country.

Kerry's words became emblematic of the Vietnam War: "Someone has to die so that President Nixon won't be, and these are his words, 'the first President to lose a war.' We are asking Americans to think about that, because how do you ask a man to be the last man to die in Vietnam? How do you ask a man to be the last man to die for a mistake?"[6]

Winter Soldier 2008

Thirty-seven years after the Vietnam winter soldiers bore witness to the atrocities of that illegal war, another group of traumatized soldiers bared their souls and described the atrocities they had experienced in the Iraq and Afghanistan wars. More than 200 men and women joined together in a collective unburdening of grief and guilt. It was a catharsis for the participants.

This time Winter Soldier was sponsored by the Iraq Veterans Against the War (IVAW) and was held at the National Labor College outside of Washington, DC. The four-day event was called Winter Soldier: Iraq and Afghanistan—Eyewitness Accounts of the Occupation. Although widely covered by the alternative press, the hearings were largely ignored by the corporate media. Some of the testimony is presented in *Winter Soldier: Iraq and Afghanistan*, a book by IVAW and Aaron Glantz.[7] Some is available on Web sites such as DemocracyNow.org.

IVAW put a great deal of effort into organizing the event. It got assistance from mental health professionals, who developed a national network of therapists willing to provide counseling for witnesses at Winter Soldier and afterward. The National Lawyers Guild's Military Law Task Force (MLTF) agreed to assemble a legal team, which advised witnesses before they testified.

IVAW's three unifying principles are the immediate withdrawal of all U.S. troops from Iraq and Afghanistan; reparations for the Iraqi people; and consistent, reliable medical care for all veterans of these wars. The organization maintains that the abuse at Abu Ghraib prison and the massacre at Haditha are not isolated incidents perpetrated by a few bad apples, as the Pentagon claimed. They are part of a pattern of an increasingly bloody occupation. In keeping with these principles, a number of witnesses also testified about the military's crimes against its own, particularly the failure to provide adequate medical care to soldiers injured or made ill in combat and the failure to protect women soldiers in Iraq and elsewhere from sexual assault by other soldiers.

Former Sgt. Logan Laituri, who served in the U.S. Army in Iraq from 2004 to 2005 before he was discharged as a conscientious objector, testified, "The problem that we face in Iraq is that policy makers in leadership have set a precedent of lawlessness where we don't abide by the rule of law, we don't respect international treaties, so when that atmosphere exists it lends itself to criminal activity."[8]

Perry O'Brien, an Afghanistan veteran and organizer of the event, cited one purpose of Winter Soldier as the unburdening of guilt: "But the disconnect between the [soldiers'] code and what soldiers are asked to do in the war is the source of a tremendous amount of guilt that many of us carry around. Kids grow up wanting to be GI Joe and save lives. But military policy is dictating that people do terrible things, things that violate their conscience, and then have the psychological burden of carrying that around, because the military says you can't talk about it. Soldiers live with it and die with it."[9]

Adam Kokesh, IVAW's cochair, said, "There are too many veterans returning from futile occupations with heads full of lies and hearts full of sorrow. Minds full of bad memories and bodies full of shrapnel. Fists full of anger and families full of confusion. It's not a strong place from which to make yourself politically relevant. But out of a strong sense of duty, some of us are trying to put our experiences to use for a good cause. Some of us couldn't live with ourselves if we weren't doing everything we could to bring our brothers and sisters home as soon as possible."[10]

"We were not bad people," said Cliff Hicks, a 23-year-old Iraq veteran, reflecting the sentiments of many other speakers. "We were all good people in a bad situation, and we did what we had to do to get through."[11]

IVAW's executive director, Kelly Dougherty, served in Iraq in

2003 as a military police officer. "It's not going to be easy to hear what we have to say," she warned the audience. "It's not going to be easy for us to tell it. But we believe that the only way this war is going to end is if the American people truly understand what we have done in their name."[12]

Veterans spoke about shootings and beatings of children and other innocent civilians as well as the torture of prisoners. Several described carrying "drop weapons" (weapons or tools to plant on the bodies of Iraqi civilians who were wrongfully killed).

Ian J. Lavalle, who served in Iraq in 2005, reported, "We dehumanized people. The way we spoke about them, the way we destroyed their livelihoods, their families, doing raids, manhandling them, throwing the men on the ground while their family was crying... I became a person I never thought I would become. It really upset me that I did these things." Lavalle was honorably discharged from the Army after he attempted suicide.[13]

Jon Michael Turner began by telling the audience, "Once a Marine, always a Marine," and he tossed his dog tags into the audience, saying, "Fuck you, I don't work for you no more." His first confirmed kill was on April 18, 2006, when he shot an Iraqi boy in front of his father. It took two shots to kill the boy. Turner had a photo of the boy's open skull. His commanding officer congratulated Turner, then offered a four-day pass to anyone who got a kill by stabbing an enemy. Turner concluded, "I am sorry for the hate and destruction that I have inflicted on innocent people. I am sorry for the things I did. I am no longer the monster that I once was."[14] Turner said that "any time we did have embedded reporters with us, our actions would change drastically."[15]

Patrick Dougherty, who served in Iraq for 14 months beginning in 2003, said he "felt from the start that we had no intention to win the hearts and minds. The way we treated our detainees like animals, kept them in cages in the hot sun all day." Former Marine Bryan Casler recalled how his fellow Marines urinated and defecated into food and then gave it to Iraqi children.[16]

Jason Hurd told of his experience in Iraq in 2004. "Individuals from my unit indiscriminately and unnecessarily opened fire on innocent civilians as they're driving down the road on their own streets." Hurd is still haunted by the image of a man running toward him, carrying a 17- or 18-year-old, a thin, pale Iraqi man. The man was missing part of his arm, bones were protruding, and shrapnel wounds covered his torso. "I noticed that his entire left butt cheek was missing," Hurd reported, "and it was bleeding profusely, and it was pooling blood. And to this day, I have that image burned in my mind's eye. Almost every couple of days, I will get a flash of red color in my mind's eye, and it won't have any shape, no form, just a flash of red. And every time, I associate it with that instance. So not only are we disrupting the lives of Iraqi civilians, we're disrupting the lives of our veterans with this occupation."[17]

Jason Moon gave a horrific account of the treatment of Iraqi children by U.S. soldiers. He described an incident in which an Iraqi man was selling soda out of a motorcycle to soldiers, and a seven- or eight-year-old child was in the sidecar. "When the man refused to go away, the MP on patrol put him to the ground with a gun to his head and started stripping his vehicle and searching it. They then took the child, picked it up into the air, and threw it full force onto the ground. I didn't see the child get up." Moon showed a video clip with his sergeant declaring, "The difference between an insurgent and an Iraqi civilian is whether they are dead or alive."[18]

Clifton Hicks served as a tank driver in the Army in 2003 and 2004. He recalled with horror watching as a warplane strafed a five-building apartment complex full of civilians, riddling it with gunfire.[19]

Hart Viges joined the Army shortly after 9/11 and was part of the invasion of Iraq in March 2003. He admitted "laying down mortar fire on this town full of people." But Viges "never really saw the effects of my mortar rounds in the towns. So that just leaves my imagination open to countless deaths that I don't know how many civilians, innocents I've killed, helped kill." Viges was ordered by his lieutenant colonel to fire on all taxicabs. "Excuse me? Did I hear you right? Fire on all taxicabs?" Viges asked. "You heard me, trooper," his superior replied. "Fire on all taxicabs."[20]

Jason Washburn supplemented Viges's story about taxicabs: "And most of the innocents that I actually saw get killed were behind the wheel of a vehicle, usually a taxi driver. I've been present for almost a dozen of those types of people that got killed just driving."[21]

Vincent Emanuelli described with disgust the way American soldiers treated the Iraqi dead: "Standard operating procedure was to run over them or take pictures."[22]

Mike Totten was deployed to Iraq in April 2003 and returned home one year later. His remarks summed up what many at these hearings were feeling. "My being here displays my anger, both by— on multiple levels—by the Americans' behavior overseas, by our president's continuous rhetoric about Iraq being a success, about this country's citizens, an apathy to this occupation," Totten explained. "And this is why I'm here today, as well. These events happen in our name, and each and every single one of you are responsible for this, as well. I am very sorry for my actions, and I can't take back what I did. I ask the forgiveness of the people of Iraq and of my country, and I will not enable this any further."[23]

The statements of these troops were moving, dramatic, and heart-wrenching. But some of the most poignant testimony came from the mother and father of Corporal Jeffrey Michael Lucey, who described their son's life—and death—after he returned from Iraq in 2003. "Our Marine physically returned to us, but his spirit died somewhere in Iraq," Joyce Lucey said. "As we celebrated his homecoming, Jeff masked the anger, the guilt, the confusion, pain, and darkness that are part of the hidden wounds of war behind his smile."

Joyce said that Jeff vomited just about every day after his return up until the day he died. On Christmas Eve, after he had been drinking, Jeff grabbed his dog tags, tossed them to his sister, and called himself a murderer. He was depressed and suffered from panic attacks, nightmares, and a poor appetite. The Department of Veterans Affairs called it classic post-traumatic stress disorder (PTSD). "Our days consisted of constant fear, apprehension, helplessness, while we watched this young man being consumed by this cancer that ravaged his soul," Jeff's mom recalled. "I sat on the deck with this person who was impersonating my son and listened to him while he recounted bits and pieces of his time in Iraq. Then he would grind his fist into his hand, and he'd say, 'You could never understand.'"

Jeff's dad, Kevin Lucey, continued the story. "Jeffrey asked me, for the second time within the past 10 days, if he could just sit in my lap and I could rock him for about—well, for a while. And we did. We sat there for about 45 minutes, and I was rocking Jeff, and we were in total silence. As his private therapist that we had hired said, it was his last harbor and his last place of refuge. The next day, I came home. It was about quarter after seven. I held Jeff one last time, as I lowered his body from the rafters and took the hose from around his neck."[24]

Rules of Engagement

The law of war, which is set forth in the Hague Conventions and Geneva Conventions, is incorporated into U.S. law through the

Constitution. Civilians must be protected. Attacks that might harm civilians or hospitals, schools, or places of worship must not be excessive in relation to the anticipated military advantage. The United States must promulgate rules of engagement (ROE) that set forth guidelines and place limitations on the use of force to ensure its lawful use.

Several GIs at Winter Soldier 2008 testified that they were subject to amorphous and contradictory rules of engagement—often free-fire zones where they could shoot at anything that moved. These rules, or lack thereof, led to the commission of atrocities and war crimes.

"During the course of my three tours, the rules of engagement changed a lot. It seemed like every time we turned around we had different rules of engagement," Jason Washburn testified. "And they told us the reasons they were changing them was because it depended on the climate of the area at the time, what the threat level was deemed to be. And the higher the threat level was, the more viciously we were permitted and expected to respond."

Washburn added that during the invasion they were ordered to use "target identification" before engaging with anyone. But if the town or city was a known threat, "we were allowed to shoot whatever we wanted. It was deemed to be a free-fire zone ... Any that we saw, everything that we saw, we engaged it and opened fire on everything... There was really no rule governing the amount of force we were allowed to use on targets during the invasion." Washburn recalled a woman with a huge bag who looked as though she was headed toward them. "So we lit her up with the Mark 19, which is an automatic grenade launcher. And when the dust settled, we realized that the bag was only full of groceries. And I mean, she had been trying to bring us food, and we blew her to pieces for it."[25]

"If there were thirty or less civilians, we were allowed to fire into the area. If there were over thirty, we were supposed to take fire and send it up the chain of command. These were the rules of engagement," said Jason Moon.[26]

"We just basically changed [the rules] ourselves," Corporal Garret Reppenhagen, who served in the Army in Iraq in 2004 and 2005, reported. The soldiers got no briefings on the rules of engagement; the rules were left up to individual units.[27] "You're not concerned with the rules of engagement and the Geneva Conventions. Your primary concern is getting yourself and your buddies home alive." He said the attitude in his company was "We didn't get in trouble for that? Oh, let's try this."[28]

Logan Laituri testified that his unit's rules of engagement were verbal only: "Signal, Shout, Show [weapon], Shove, Shoot." His unit was authorized to use its weapons any time the troops felt threatened.[29]

Sgt. Jason Lemieux, a Marine who served three tours of duty in Iraq, said his commander's order was "Kill those who need to be killed and save those who need to be saved." Anyone who stepped outside a door was shot, and anyone with a shovel or standing on a roof with a cell phone was considered a hostile target. "The rules of engagement were broadly defined and loosely enforced . . . Anyone who tells you differently is a liar or a fool. [The rules] were gradually reduced to a case of nonexistence."[30]

In April 2004 in an apparent act of retaliation and collective punishment for the killing and mutilation of four Blackwater Security Consulting mercenaries in Fallujah, Iraq, the U.S. military attacked and killed scores of civilians. The Fourth Geneva Convention forbids collective punishment. "During the siege of Fallujah," Adam Kokesh said, "we changed our rules of engagement more often then we changed our underwear."[31]

The Military Law Task Force filed a Freedom of Information Act (FOIA) request to obtain the rules of engagement under which the U.S. military operated during its 2004 assaults on Fallujah and the 2005 shooting attack on a car carrying Italian journalist Giuliana Sgrena to the Baghdad airport.

The U.S. military's siege of Fallujah resulted in the deaths of at least several thousand civilians, if not tens of thousands, and the displacement of approximately a quarter of the city's 400,000 residents. Numerous reports told of residents being shot and killed by U.S. snipers upon exiting their homes, without any justification or basis. Journalists reported the use of white phosphorous gas and massive aerial bombings, some of which included the use of illegal cluster bombs that discharge shrapnel, which slices through houses and buildings and kills the inhabitants while leaving the structures standing.

After the siege the U.S. military, in an apparent assassination attempt, attacked Giuliana Sgrena, the only unembedded Western journalist who was covering the destruction of the city, by firing upon her car, wounding her, and killing an Italian government agent, whose last act was to throw his body over her, saving her.

In response to the FOIA request, the government released only general guidelines that set forth the escalation of force as "Shout, Show, Shove, Shoot." The MLTF still has not received the context or scenario of that escalation. For example, if a U.S. soldier asks an Iraqi civilian to sit down on the curb and that civilian does not comply after a shout and shove, the guidelines are not clear about whether the ROE authorizes the soldier to kill absent any other reason.

On April 28, 2008, U.S. District Court Judge Marilyn Hall Patel rejected the government's attempts to continue withholding documents from the MLTF and refused to accept what she characterized as the government's "trust us" doctrine. As the book goes to press, it is unclear what information will eventually be released and whether it will come close to explaining how any justification for the massive civilian casualties, indiscriminate killing and aerial bombings in Fallujah, and the shooting attack on the car carrying journalist Sgrena can be legally supported.

Winter Soldier Goes to Congress

Two months after the 2008 Winter Soldier hearings, several veterans testified before the Congressional Progressive Caucus on Capitol Hill. Nine of the veterans had served in Iraq, and one had served in Afghanistan. About 40 veterans were in the audience. "We now have an opportunity to hear not from the military's top brass but directly from you, the very soldiers who put your lives on the line to carry out this president's failed policies," the caucus cochair, Congresswoman Lynn Woolsey (D-CA), told the witnesses.[32]

Former Capt. Luis Carlos Montalvan, who served directly under Army Gen. David Petraeus in 2005 and 2006, reported that he witnessed U.S. military personnel carry out waterboarding, which is a torture technique. Torture is a war crime. Those who commit war crimes and their commanders can be held liable under the War Crimes Act. Under the well-established doctrine of command responsibility, if the commander knew or should have known that his subordinates would commit war crimes and did nothing to stop or prevent it, he or she is equally culpable.

"I was ordered multiple times by commissioned officers and noncommissioned officers to shoot unarmed civilians if their presence made me uncomfortable," one of the veterans, Jason Lemieux, told the panel. "These orders were given with the understanding that my immediate chain of command would protect our subordinates from legal repercussions."[33]

Former Sgt. Kristofer Shawn Goldsmith testified that he enlisted in the Army at the age of 18, just after high school graduation. Goldsmith, who saw the World Trade Center tower collapse, said, "[I] knew full well that I would quickly be sent to Iraq. Like many other Americans at the time I was still under the influence of the media and its terrorism paranoia, and believed that somewhere in the deserts of Iraq were thousands of weapons of mass destruction (WMDs)." Upon his arrival in Sadr City, Goldsmith learned that "we were not being greeted as 'liberators' by the civilian populace, but as an oppressive occupying force." He saw graffiti that read "Welcome, America, to the Second Vietnam."[34]

Much like Dr. Howard Levy four decades before, Goldsmith saw through the alleged "humanitarian" aid drops. Goldsmith knew that they were really effectuated to "win the hearts and minds of the people, . . . military missions used only as a tool aimed at accomplishing the goal of making Iraqis believe that we were there to help them." But, said Goldsmith, "we never provided any real medical supplies, despite the fact that the hospitals and clinics in the area were in dire need of antibiotics and basic surgical equipment."

Goldsmith described his diagnosis of PTSD and subsequent suicide attempt. The note he wrote after ingesting about a dozen Percocet pills and a heavy dose of vodka read, "Stop-loss killed me" and "End stop-loss now." Fortunately, the military police at Fort Stewart found Goldsmith, rushed him to the hospital, and saved his life.[35]

After the hearing Sgt. Matthis Chiroux, a member of the Individual Ready Reserve (IRR), who served four years in the Army until being honorably separated from active duty, announced his intention to refuse orders to return to active duty and deploy to Iraq. "Thanks in great part to the truths of war being fearlessly spoken by my fellow IVAW members," Chiroux said, "I stand before you today with the strength, clarity, and resolve to declare to the military and the world that this soldier will not be deploying to Iraq. This occupation is unconstitutional and illegal, and I hereby lawfully refuse to participate, as I will surely be a party to war crimes."[36] In mid-2008, 13 members of the House of Representatives wrote to President Bush expressing their support for service members who oppose the war in Iraq; they mentioned Chiroux's action and expressed support for all military members who speak out or otherwise support efforts to bring all the troops home. In November Chiroux received notice from the Army that he faced misconduct discharge, potentially an other than honorable discharge.

So far, none of the Winter Soldier witnesses have been prosecuted for their testimony, though some active duty witnesses were harassed by superiors. The MLTF has agreed to assist if legal action is taken against any of the witnesses. Those who testified adhered to regulations carefully during their statements, and as one MLTF organizer noted, an effort to charge them with military or civilian offenses would cause difficulties for the military. Nonetheless, the soldiers and veterans who testified in Winter Soldier have taken very real risks to tell the American public the truth. Chapter 4 discusses the political rights of military personnel, including the right to free speech, but also details the military's continuing efforts to limit those rights.

FOUR

Dissent and Disengagement

RESISTANCE TO MILITARY POLICIES takes many forms. In addition to refusal of orders and conscientious objection, GIs have used demonstrations, picket lines, rallies, petitions to Congress, street theater, statements to the media and the public, long visits to Canada, underground newspapers, discharge requests, and other means to disengage from the current wars. Dissent has manifested in as many ways as there are soldiers with imaginations, and 21st-century technology offers a number of new ways to voice that dissent. The current movement among GIs and veterans includes a remarkable blend of old and new methods, giving voice to a traditional message with important modern additions.

This chapter documents one of the cases that have put dissent, and particularly free speech, in the news. First Lieutenant Ehren Watada, who refused in a very public way to deploy with his Army unit, explained his reasons and objections, and was court-martialed, in part for speaking his mind. We also explain some of the other ways in which GIs and veterans have disengaged, particularly from the war in Iraq, and examine the military's heavy-handed response to even the most legal forms of dissent. We explore the Vietnam-era GI movement as the origin of many forms of dissent and also new methods made available by modern technology. Finally, this chapter offers a practical explanation of the law and regulations governing dissent and procedures for "redress of grievances" in the military.

The Constitution allows service members the right to dissent, with some limitations that are surprising to civilians. More often than not, methods of dissent have been tested in public and then in the courts before making their way into military regulations. Some soldiers choose ways to dissent that are well within the boundaries of the regs. Others skirt those boundaries. Indeed, creative GIs and their legal supporters often redraw the boundaries as they go. All of these approaches have impact—on Pentagon policy makers, Congress, the president, the public, other GIs and their families, or all of the above.

This dissent is honorable, in the tradition of soldiers who fought foreign occupation in the Revolutionary War, of those who marched in the streets in a massive bring-them-home movement after World War II, and of those who refused to march out into the fields of Vietnam. In this and subsequent chapters, we demonstrate that many soldiers and veterans of the current wars and occupations find themselves faced with a duty and need to dissent. Although the form and consequences may vary, all are acts of disengagement—from the wars, from illegal military policies, and in some cases from the military itself.

Contested Territory: Free Speech and the Duty to Speak Out

In June 2006 First Lieutenant Ehren Watada became the first commissioned officer to publicly disobey an order to deploy to Iraq. Following his commander's instruction to "know everything there is to know about your mission, not just where you're shooting the missiles but why you're shooting the missiles," Watada began to read about Iraq. The result, he said in one of his public statements, was that "I realized we had been lied to." [1]

The turning point for Lieutenant Watada came when he "saw the pain and suffering of so many soldiers and their families, and innocent Iraqis." At a June 7, 2006, press conference in Tacoma, Washington, he said, "I best serve my soldiers by speaking out against unlawful orders of the highest levels of my chain of command, and making sure our leaders are held accountable." Lieutenant Watada felt he "had the obligation to step up and do whatever it takes," even if that meant facing court-martial and imprisonment.[2]

Some of the charges against Lieutenant Watada were based on his statements about the war. At his press conference, he said, "The war in Iraq is in fact illegal. It is my obligation and my duty to refuse any orders to participate in this war. An order to take part in an illegal war is unlawful in itself. So my obligation is not to follow the order to go to Iraq."

Citing "deception and manipulation . . . and willful misconduct by the highest levels of my chain of command," Lieutenant Watada declared that there is "no greater betrayal to the American people" than the Iraq war. Rejecting an attempt to settle the case informally, the Army charged Lieutenant Watada with missing movement and conduct unbecoming an officer and a gentleman. The second charge stemmed from his public statements; in the military scheme of things, he had acted improperly by discussing the legality of the war with reporters and at a convention of Veterans for Peace.

At Lieutenant Watada's court-martial, held in February 2007, military judge John Head refused to allow expert testimony, including testimony by Marjorie Cohn, on the illegality of the

Iraq war and the war crimes the Bush administration was committing there. Ironically, later developments in the case may put that testimony at issue again.

The court-martial ended when, well into the trial, Judge Head rejected a pretrial agreement. In the agreement both sides had acknowledged that Lieutenant Watada missed his deployment. Lieutenant Watada said the acknowledgment was not a guilty plea, because he believed the war was illegal, so the order to deploy was unlawful. But the judge thought that it was virtually an admission of guilt, and thus he could no longer accept the agreement. Over defense objection the judge then declared a mistrial.

Defense attorneys argued that no second court-martial could take place without a breach of the Double Jeopardy Clause of the Fifth Amendment to the U.S. Constitution and a violation of the Uniform Code of Military Justice, but two military appeals courts rejected those arguments. Lieutenant Watada's attorneys then filed a petition for a writ of habeas corpus in the U.S. District Court for the Western District of Washington at Tacoma.

On October 22, 2008, Judge Benjamin Settle agreed with Lieutenant Watada's double jeopardy claim and dismissed three of the five counts against him. As this book goes to press, the Army has not decided whether to pursue the remaining counts, which charged Lieutenant Watada with conduct unbecoming an officer. The counts involve speech issues and may again raise the question of expert witness testimony on the legality of the war.

One of Lieutenant Watada's attorneys, Kenneth Kagan, told the authors, "I see Ehren Watada as an American hero because he took extremely seriously the oath he swore as an officer of the United States Army to uphold and defend the Constitution of the United States. He believed in 2005–06, and continues to believe today, that an officer has the duty to understand the nature of any assignment in which he is expected to participate, including the culture and history of any country to which his commanders may send him, the nature of the conflict in which the United States armed forces may be engaged, as well as the lawfulness of orders he receives. The Army, in fact, teaches those very principles to its officers."

Kagan added, "Lieutenant Watada's heroism arose in his conclusion that the invasion of Iraq was unlawful, that his participation in that unlawful invasion would abet an unlawful war of aggression, and that he would be willing to accept the consequences of his refusal to participate, despite great personal sacrifices, including nearly total alienation from his comrades-in-arms, the potential for a lengthy prison term, and the hatred and scorn heaped upon him by untold numbers of misguided citizens. I have been deeply moved by his courage and steadfastness throughout."

Although some were critical, Lieutenant Watada found other officers and enlisted personnel supportive not only of his message but of the fact that he felt a duty to speak out. Many who disagreed with him emphasized their respect for his right to speak his mind—and his duty to do so if he believed his orders were wrong. Courage to Resist (a national organization supporting military resisters), Iraq Veterans Against the War, and a committee of Lieutenant Watada's supporters held demonstrations outside the main gate to Fort Lewis during the court-martial. They waved and flashed victory *V*s at detractors who made rude gestures. On and off base, soldiers and their families talked about the case and considered what they should or should not do about the war.

Pablo Paredes, Ehrren Watada, the Winter Soldier witnesses, and many other soldiers and sailors have spoken publicly against the wars and occupation. According to Maj. John L. Kiel Jr., "Remarks against the president have become more prevalent among service members because they communicate through a host of mediums unfathomable to yesterday's generation."[3] In an institution that values conformity and often sees it as evidence of discipline, simply voicing dissident ideas is a strong form of protest.

In theory, military personnel have the right to express their dissent, a right grounded in the First Amendment and set out in military regulations. These regulations acknowledge rights to free speech, protest, and assembly, with limitations; they are the result of soldiers' persistent demands for these rights over several decades. Nevertheless, even speech and actions that are clearly protected, such as petitions to members of Congress, run the risk of informal and extralegal reprisals, discussed later in this chapter.

Some service members, veterans, and their families have created collective antiwar statements designed to allow many service members to speak with one voice. Petitions and letter-writing campaigns demonstrate that the signers' views are shared by many others, an important counter to the military's claims that outspoken critics within the ranks, like Pablo Paredes and Katherine Jashinski, are rare exceptions to most soldiers' views.

In 2006 a group of active duty soldiers and sailors planned a creative campaign to express their opposition to the Iraq war to Congress and the public. They conferred with other soldiers and activists, including perhaps most notably David Cortright, author of *Soldiers in Revolt: The American Military Today*. They consulted attorneys, including J. E. McNeil at the Center on Conscience and War, to help develop a strategy that complied with military regulations. The result was the online Appeal for Redress (at www .appealforredress.org):

> As a patriotic American proud to serve the nation in uniform, I respectfully urge my political leaders in Congress to support the

prompt withdrawal of all American military forces and bases from Iraq. Staying in Iraq will not work and is not worth the price. It is time for U.S. troops to come home.

Many progressive sites, blogs, and online newsletters mentioned the appeal and offered a link to it. Media interest was considerable—organizers discussed it in *Navy Times*, on *60 Minutes*, and in the *Nation*. The Appeal for Redress was first presented during the Martin Luther King Jr. Day weekend, with a press conference on January 15, 2007, and formal presentation to Rep. Dennis Kucinich and other supportive members of Congress the next day. At that point, the appeal had over 1,000 signatures.

The Web site appealforredress.org states that it plans to accept signatures until all active duty, national guard, and reserve troops are withdrawn from Iraq. Soldiers continue to add their signatures, and as of January 29, 2009, the number stood at 2,230 names. As one might expect, the official reaction to the appeal was that the numbers were insignificant. But those who signed the appeal were simply the tip of the iceberg of dissenters. "For everyone who has heard about the appeal," said IVAW executive director Kelly Dougherty, "there are so many dozens of others who agree with it but have not heard about it, or agree with it but are intimidated by the military."[4]

High-Visibility: Demonstrations, Protests, and Street Theater

Members of IVAW, Veterans for Peace, and Vietnam Veterans Against the War, in particular, are visible as speakers and demonstrators at antiwar rallies and marches around the country, sometimes joined by GIs along the way. Speaking as veterans, their voices and presence carry considerable weight, reminding watchers of the extensive antiwar sentiment in the military. In national demonstrations called by United for Peace and Justice (UFPJ) and Act Now to Stop War and End Racism (ANSWER), a contingent of veterans and GIs has been front and center at the head of marches. IVAW, along with other veterans and military family groups, has taken to heart the importance of a GI movement as a strong element in the broader antiwar movement. IVAW actively recruits service members and focuses many of its actions on GIs. It encouraged soldiers to attend the Winter Soldier hearings, whether or not they wished to testify.

In early 2007 IVAW conducted Operation First Casualty. Using dramatic street theater, veterans dressed in military jackets and camouflage conducted combat patrols on the streets of downtown Manhattan; Washington, DC; Chicago; and elsewhere. They detained suspected hostiles (other IVAW members), ordered or forced them to lie down, then restrained them with flexible handcuffs and pulled cloth bags over their heads. The "soldiers" watched for sniper fire, conducted vehicle searches, and shouted orders over the heads of the crowd as they moved from street to street. Bystanders and television audiences watching their local news got a vivid and frightening picture of the reality in Iraqi cities.

In 2007 and 2008, IVAW organized bus tours and "engagements" at major military bases in which they met and talked to soldiers and their families. The organizers spent several days at each base, handing out leaflets at the front gates, giving away copies of the film *Sir! No Sir!*, and recruiting new members. They offered GIs information about the GI Rights Network for guidance on discharges and other legal matters. At Fort Benning, in Georgia, IVAW members were detained for allegedly walking onto the base, and elsewhere MPs called civilian police to remove them from public sidewalks outside the gates. After each engagement at a base, the IVAW office received new membership applications from soldiers stationed there.

In February 2008 a group of soldiers engaged in a "blitz," plastering areas of Killeen, Texas, with pamphlets about the war in Iraq and soldiers' rights. Killeen, the base community near Fort Hood, was home to the Oleo Strut coffeehouse (named after a shock absorber), a place of relaxation for soldiers during the Vietnam War. On July 22, 2008, veterans of the Oleo Strut and other vets and supporters announced plans to open a new coffeehouse, to be called Under the Hood. Another coffeehouse, Coffee Strong (a play on the Army's "Army strong" recruiting ads) opened outside Fort Lewis in Washington State in November 2008. A Different Drummer, near Fort Drum in upstate New York, is the third and oldest Iraq-era coffeehouse for soldiers.

Squelching Dissent

Many GI protesters face repercussions from their commands. Military officials have a hard time accepting the notion of dissent, and some officers rankle at the protections offered protesters and outspoken soldiers in Department of Defense (DoD) Directive 1325.6, Guidelines for Handling Dissident and Protest Activities among Members of the Armed Forces. When resisters clearly violate the UCMJ by refusing orders or by going AWOL and speaking out publicly, commanders are happy to follow the disciplinary rules, usually with much greater zeal than they apply to cases of soldiers who go AWOL for personal reasons. Commands almost always punish political dissidents more severely than they do soldiers who have other reasons for skipping duty.

But commands don't always give up, even when the picket lines or speeches look quite proper under the regulations and when their attorneys tell commanders that prosecutions won't fly. Some commanders ignore the warnings and press charges against GIs who talk to reporters or who are seen marching in demonstrations. And in some cases their overreaction has strengthened or expanded the rights that anger them.

Some commanding officers adhere strictly to the law and respect soldiers' constitutional rights, but GI activists can expect that their actions will be closely scrutinized. If off-base picketers wander too near the base's property lines, or if speeches come a little too close to disrespect for the commander in chief, service members can expect prosecution. If their actions are well within the boundaries of the regs, GIs often receive formal warnings that sound remarkably like, but aren't quite, orders to desist.

During the Operation First Casualty action in Washington, DC, IVAW member Adam Kokesh, a Marine combat veteran, wore a military uniform without his name and rank. Weeks later, Kokesh and two other IVAW members received warnings from the Marine Corps Mobilization Command that they faced misconduct discharge from the reserves for antiwar activities in which they wore parts of military uniforms.

Kokesh and the two others, like many IVAW members, had finished their active duty service but were required to remain in the Individual Ready Reserve (IRR, or inactive reserve) for the remainder of their standard eight-year military obligation. IRR members do not attend drills or perform duties, but they are subject to call-up for active duty during military mobilizations. The Marine Corps Mobilization Command notified the three that they were being recommended for other than honorable discharges from the IRR.

Each of these IRR Marines had received an honorable separation from the Marine Corps after active duty and combat service in Iraq. The Marine Corps could not change those separations and would have had great difficulty pressing charges under the UCMJ, but the Mobilization Command believed it could discharge them from the IRR itself for misconduct. A misconduct discharge allows administrative action against service members whose conduct would have been a violation of the UCMJ, whether or not they had been charged with any offense. In one case, the misconduct was based on public comments made by Liam Madden, one of the three reservists, and one of the organizers of the Appeal for Redress. They were alleged to be "disloyal statements" in violation of Article 134 of the UCMJ, which prohibits, among other things, "all disorders and neglects to the prejudice of good order and discipline in the armed forces" and "all conduct of a nature to bring discredit upon the armed forces." In fact, Madden had said that the president's administration was guilty of war crimes, that the Iraq war was a war of aggression and empire building, and that the president had betrayed U.S. military personnel, "or words to that effect." Discharge from the IRR had never been used against political demonstrators. Civil rights organizations were shocked at the attempt, which angered even conservative veterans groups. The Marine Corps realized it had made a blunder.

Of the three reservists, one was on disability after service, and all of them were reasonably concerned about the possible future effects on their comrade's medical benefits. The Marine Corps offered to drop the whole matter if he would agree not to wear a uniform in public, and he did so. Kokesh and Madden demanded the right to a hearing before a Marine administrative discharge board. After his hearing Kokesh was awarded a general discharge under honorable conditions. When Kokesh's attorney spoke to the media about possible litigation, the Marine Corps recognized its vulnerability. The Mobilization Command wrote to Madden, offering to drop the discharge proceedings if he would make a verbal promise not to wear the uniform at demonstrations. He wrote back saying that he would do so "upon receiving a signed, written statement on official

USMC letterhead acknowledging that my statements in question were neither disloyal nor inaccurate."[5] The Marine Corps dropped his discharge proceedings without a response to his letter or any further comments about uniforms or statements.

If GIs' dissent is just too legal for any chance of successful disciplinary action, commands often look for other reasons to take disciplinary steps. Soldiers who make protests find that haircut regulations are applied to them with enthusiasm, that their tendency to be five minutes late after lunch like the rest of their unit is suddenly not acceptable. Health and welfare inspections (searches of lockers and living spaces in barracks or on board ships) and random drug searches may increase after GIs attend a rally.

Informal reprisals, harassment, and allegedly unrelated personnel actions are common as well. Dissidents often receive lower performance evaluations or less pleasant assignments than their coworkers. These are discretionary matters—assigning protesters more deck-swabbing or clean-up duty than others isn't illegal, only doing so because they are protesters. Recipients of arbitrary actions of this sort can challenge them successfully only if they can prove the improper motives behind them. While he was still on active duty, Sergeant Liam Madden spoke to the press about the Appeal for Redress and the war in Iraq and held workshops about the politics of the war on his base in Quantico, Virginia. His command "just gave me lousy jobs and told all my peers they were not allowed to talk to Sergeant Madden. It was a pretty lonely time," he told a reporter.[6]

Not all who protest are punished, however. After Sergeant Ronn Cantu signed a petition to Congress demanding U.S. withdrawal from Iraq and gave interviews to *Democracy Now!*, *60 Minutes*, and *Inter Press*, he was promoted to staff sergeant. Cantu had also launched an online forum called ASoldiersVoice.net.

New Technology and Traditional Dissent

The Internet has given service members tools of resistance that were unimaginable during the Vietnam War. Online newsletters like *GI Special* (at www.militaryproject.org) include signed and anonymous letters and articles from GIs, many of them in Iraq or Afghanistan, along with articles by family members, veterans, and other civilian supporters. IVAW's Web site, IVAW.org, serves a similar function; it has notes and comments from GIs and veterans in addition to news reports and frequent updates on IVAW activities, profiles of some members, and news or opinion letters from members and supporters. Courage to Resist regularly updates its Web site, CouragetoResist.org, with a list of public resisters and news about resistance. Antiwar blogs by named and anonymous soldiers flourish. Although individual service members who speak out might be vulnerable to retaliation from their commands, the collective production of online newsletters and anonymous blogs affords some practical protection, much like that of the unsigned underground newspapers produced during the Vietnam era.

Some antiwar GI bloggers have been challenged, however. A few have been reprimanded or told that their blogs may be illegal; others have been warned that even general information about Iraq or Afghanistan may violate ambiguous regulations on classified information. Still other soldiers have been encouraged to post prowar images on YouTube.

Using the System to Protect Dissent: Vietnam

In 1972 as the Navy's role in the Vietnam War expanded, a little book was written for a class on GI rights and military counseling for enlisted personnel and civilian supporters in San Diego. The class was taught by members of the Center for Servicemen's Rights and the National Lawyers Guild. Some of the unnamed authors' own military stories appeared in the book. In 148 pages, *Turning the Regs Around* discussed a wide range of topics, from demonstrations to grievances and complaints to discharges.[7] The book summed up the experiences of individual GIs and GI antiwar and black power organizations in the United States, Germany, and Asia throughout the course of the war. It explained regulations and applicable articles of the UCMJ, reprinted excerpts from military legal manuals, pamphlets and leaflets prepared by GI counseling groups, and offered practical suggestions and sample complaints for redress of grievances under Article 138 of the UCMJ.

In its first chapter, *Turning the Regs Around* discussed the importance of regulations protecting dissent and the role of the GI movement in gaining these rights:

> Up until the last few years, the brass has been able to ignore [service members'] rights pretty much at will. But lately, people have been standing up and fighting—on ships and bases around the world and, when necessary, in the courts.
>
> Those fights have led to more rights ... But rights and laws don't always stay the same. They're changing, for better or worse, depending on whether you use, defend, and try to expand what you have or stand by and watch your rights erode away.

The book reflected the experiences and attitudes of a whole generation of soldiers, sailors, and Marines as they protested against the war, military racism, and the miserable conditions under which they worked and lived. It was reprinted, excerpted, and summarized by other GI groups and military counseling centers.

After the war the "barracks lawyer" wisdom summarized in the book was used by other dissenters and movements against oppressive military policies. The postwar efforts of African American and other minority service members to end discrimination and bigotry (discussed in Chapter 5) borrowed and expanded on the rights and regulations explained in *Turning the Regs Around*, and strengthened those rights, in turn, through their own use of the military's equal opportunity program.

As women in the military launched a new and ongoing struggle against sexual discrimination, sexual harassment, and sexual abuse (described in Chapter 6) the rights explained in the 1972 book were expanded, and new rights, like those of the Military Whistleblower Protection Act were developed, adapted, and expanded to support this movement.[8] The decades-long struggle of lesbian and gay service members and their supporters against military homophobia expanded some of those rights further in a series of federal court challenges to ever-changing discriminatory regulations, now expressed in the policy "don't ask, don't tell." These and other movements have built on the work of the GI antiwar and black power movements of the Vietnam era. Many rights these movements demanded and won then are now being strengthened and augmented in the current GI movement, and other rights remain to be taken up by the new movement.

Using the System Today:
Rules and Regulations

The law has given GI dissidents protection to speak out on a broad range of issues. The charge against Lieutenant Watada of conduct unbecoming an officer and a gentleman, which was based on antiwar statements he made in public, raises the issue of the limits of the First Amendment's protection of free speech in the military environment. While Lieutenant Watada was speaking out publicly in opposition to the war, Army Pfc. Jeremy Wilcox was speaking out publicly on the Internet in favor of racial hatred. This case provides a useful review of military law on the issue.

Wilcox was charged with violating Article 134 of the UCMJ by wrongfully advocating antigovernment and disloyal sentiments and encouraging participation in extremist organizations while identifying himself as a "U.S. Army Paratrooper" on an America Online (AOL) profile, and advocating racial intolerance by counseling and advising individuals on racist views, which, under the circumstances, resulted in prejudice to the good order and discipline of the armed forces or was of a nature to bring discredit to the armed forces. One of Wilcox's online AOL profiles stated, "We must secure the existence of our people and a future for white children." The other, an AOL Personals profile, stated that Wilcox was seeking a "female for a casual or serious relation" and identified himself as a "Pro-White activist," saying "Love your own kind and fight for your own kind."

Following Wilcox's court-martial conviction, the U.S. Court of Appeals for the Armed Forces, the highest military court, affirmed that the First Amendment "permits the expression of ideas, even the expression of ideas the vast majority of society finds offensive or distasteful." The military appellate court cited *Parker v. Levy*, in which the Supreme Court upheld Dr. Howard Levy's convictions in 1974. Regarding Levy's action of publicly urging enlisted personnel to refuse to obey orders, the high court concluded, "While the members of the military are not excluded from the protection granted by the First Amendment, the different character of the military community and of the military mission requires a different application of those protections. The fundamental necessity for obedience, and the consequent necessity for imposition of discipline, may render permissible within the military that which would be constitutionally impermissible outside it."[9]

Dangerous speech, the Wilcox court held, is speech that "interferes with or prevents the orderly accomplishment of the mission or presents a clear danger to loyalty, discipline, mission, or morale of the troops." That requires "a direct and palpable connection between speech and the military mission or military environment." If a soldier was prosecuted for speaking out against the war, the government would have to demonstrate such a nexus.

The appellate court reversed Wilcox's conviction for violation of Article 134, finding that "while repugnant," Wilcox's communications did not present "a clear danger to loyalty, discipline, mission, or morale of the troops" under the circumstances of that case. The court found no evidence that Wilcox's statements were directed at military members or ever reached his unit.[10] If the government prosecuted a soldier for posting an antiwar statement on the Internet, the prosecutor should have to prove it was read by members of his unit.

The context of the speech is important, the Wilcox appellate court said, distinguishing a case that upheld a conviction for encouraging other service members to request mast (a meeting with one's commanding officer) and refuse to fight in Vietnam. It would have been a different situation altogether if Wilcox's speech had been directed to service members. If the prosecutor had presented evidence that Wilcox's statements had been read by members of his unit or had affected the order or discipline of the Army, the case may well have come out the other way.

Military regulations can be powerful weapons for service members who choose to dissent. Service members have many more rights than the few they are taught in basic training—far more than they are told by instructors and supervisors who claim GIs give up all their rights when they sign up. The military can and does place limits on the time, place, and manner of dissident protests and speech, and it has limited control over the content. As we have shown in a number of examples, GI activists are creative in finding new legal, and sometimes not-so-legal, ways to get out their message.

DoD Directive 1325.6, Guidelines for Handling Dissent and Protest Activities among Members of the Armed Forces, describes the most basic rights for "dissident and protest activities," with guidelines concerning possession and distribution of printed materials, off-post gathering places, publication of underground newspapers, off-base demonstrations and similar activities, and GIs' attendance at those demonstrations. The regulations and related court opinions are discussed extensively elsewhere, and no short explanation can cover all of the limitations and nuances of the underlying constitutional and military law.

GIs who are considering any protest activity are encouraged to review the information on the Military Law Task Force Web site or similar sources, and those planning public or otherwise high-profile activity should generally consult a civilian attorney experienced in military law before taking action. Armed with the regulations and legal backup, service members are able to make better use of their rights and limit repercussions from commands.

The dissent regulation attempts to summarize this complex area in a few pages. It begins by explaining that the military must ensure that GIs' right to express their opinions "should be preserved to the maximum extent possible, consistent with good order and discipline and the national security," but it warns that this right must be balanced against military necessity and interests of national security. The military, being the military, tends to shift that balance toward the latter two needs, but limiting basic rights in that way is difficult. The rights protected under the Bill of Rights, statutes, and military case law and regulations cannot be contained easily in a few pages. DoD Directive 1325.6 includes caveats and limitations that are vague and somewhat confusing, particularly to lay readers. The directive tries to address the subject by speaking in the negative, explaining prohibitions and limits on the rights rather than describing the rights themselves.

This directive discusses the right to possess unauthorized material by mentioning it as an exception to the prohibition of actual or attempted distribution of material not authorized by the command. GIs must trace the language backward to read that they are free to distribute unauthorized literature off base within the United States (rules differ for GIs in foreign countries) and are free to possess on base the literature they cannot distribute there. Similarly, DoD Directive 1325.6 explains the right to participate in off-base demonstrations in the United States only by pointing out that service members may not demonstrate on base. The important issue is that participation in or attendance at off-base demonstrations is a right, unless "violence is likely to result" or the individual or demonstration actually violates the law.

The DoD directive reminds readers that commands are not allowed to "recognize or to bargain with any union representing or seeking recognition to represent service members." This provision is derived from a separate directive, DoD 1354.1, DoD Policy on Organizations That Seek to Represent or Organize Members of the Armed Forces in Negotiation or Collective Bargaining. DoD Directive 1325.6 also mentions grievances but refers readers to Article 138 of the UCMJ and the Military Whistleblowers Protection Act. This subsection of the dissent regulation ends with an important reminder to commands: "An open door policy for complaints is a basic principle of good leadership, and commanders should personally ensure that adequate procedures exist for identifying valid complaints and taking corrective action."

One last provision of DoD Directive 1325.6 discusses other prohibited activities. That section attempts to regulate participation in "organizations that espouse supremacist causes; attempt to create illegal discrimination based on race, creed, color, sex, religion or national origin; advocate the use of force or violence; or otherwise engage in efforts to deprive individuals of their civil rights." It is tied to provisions in the discharge regulations covering discharge for misconduct as well. This section was crafted specifically to deal with organizations like the Ku Klux Klan and other ultraconservative and racist groups that often try to organize on military bases; such groups and their followers have carried out vicious hate crimes against other soldiers and civilians. Its broad language could also be applied to organizations at the other end of the political spectrum and at dissident GIs whose antiwar or antiracist protests are simply labeled left-wing revolutionary actions.

Two other directives are worth noting here. DoD Directive 1334.1, Wearing of the Uniform, was used in the Marine reservists' cases mentioned earlier in this chapter. DoD Directive 1344.10, Political Activities by Members of the Armed Forces on Active Duty, limits political activity in *electoral* politics and does not apply outside of electoral politics and campaigns.

Admiral Mike Mullen, the chairman of the Joint Chiefs of Staff, wrote an unusual open letter to all uniformed military personnel before the 2008 elections, warning them not to become involved in politics. "The U.S. military must remain apolitical at all times and in all ways," Mullen declared. "It is and must always be a neutral instrument of the state, no matter what party holds sway . . . Political opinions have no place in cockpit or camp conference room."[11]

The admiral's approach was disingenuous, for he relied on the directive limiting rights in election campaigns. Written to prevent the appearance of military endorsement of candidates or their policies, and to limit a pattern of overzealous campaigning by some high-ranking officers, the directive prohibits electoral activity that is entirely proper if engaged in outside of election settings. Yet Admiral Mullen's letter suggested that service members should stay out of all politics, and should not voice opinions on any matters of government or political policy. Although the cockpit may not be a forum to debate presidential candidates, pilots may freely express their views on the war, if the regulations are honored. Soldiers are not required or encouraged to obey blindly, without questioning orders and the policies underlying them. As Lieutenant Watada said, service members have a duty to look for the truth and to speak out when policies are illegal or wrong. Rules of disengagement are as important for honorable soldiers as the rules of engagement must be in the field.

An important weapon in the GI arsenal of dissent is Article 138 of the UCMJ, which sets out the procedure for complaints to redress grievances. Many GIs have never heard of Article 138, having been told nothing about it in trainings about the UCMJ and the military justice system. It is, however, an effective grievance procedure and one that puts control over the complaint largely in the hands of the complainants. Whether or not specific regulations have been violated, service members may complain about any wrong done to them. They begin by communicating with their commanding officer, preferably in a precomplaint letter that mentions Article 138, explains the problem, describes and attaches evidence, and requests specific redress. GIs can ask for anything from a public apology to a transfer away from an offending supervisor (it is harder to obtain the supervisor's transfer) to a reprimand of him or her.

If the commanding officer fails to act within a reasonable time or doesn't provide the relief requested, GIs can write a formal Article 138 complaint to the commanding officer's commander, similar in content to the letter but also complaining about the commander's failure to grant relief. This officer must also act within a reasonable time or become a part of the complaint. In theory Article 138 complaints can be taken to the highest levels of command.

Because they require formal responses and must be forwarded to service headquarters, Article 138 complaints tend to cause controversy and sometimes leave a black mark on a commander's record. This possibility makes commanders leery of such complaints and often ends with an odd compromise: most or all of the complaint is denied, but part or all of the redress will be given anyway. The GI gets results, and the commander doesn't look bad because the complaint was found to have no legal basis.

Complaints of any kind, even the least formal equal opportunity complaints or requests to see superiors, can lead to reprisals. Because this problem is widespread and may cause complainants a great deal of professional and legal harm, Congress required the military to create DoD Directive 7050.6, Military Whisteblower Protection, which prohibits retaliation for protected communications to Congress and proper complaints within the military system. When commands violate these provisions, the regs require a separate investigation of the reprisal and a new investigation of the original complaint. The regulations also allow expedited appeals to the service's Board for Correction of Military Records if the reprisal harms the complainant's career or creates unfavorable evaluations, reports, or other records.

GIs do in fact have the right to express their opposition to the wars verbally and in writing, share that position with the media, state it on the Internet, distribute it to other GIs in newspapers or leaflets, say it from the microphone at national antiwar rallies, and show it by marching in off-base antiwar demonstrations and picket lines. GIs have all these rights as long as they are off duty, out of uniform, and off base. They may discuss it with others in many settings on and especially off base, and may be present in coffeehouses and movement centers where it is discussed.

Although the prohibitions are numerous and important, dissident activities that remain legal offer many ways for GIs to demand that the United States get out of Iraq and Afghanistan and respect the human and civil rights of civilians and the GIs themselves. GIs may demand these things loudly, collectively, in public, in many media, and in creative new ways the GI antiwar movement of the Vietnam era could not have foreseen.

GIs, along with their families and veterans, are using these rights in increasing numbers and ways with a determination and strength that can affect the outcome of these wars. Their dissent is a critical element in disengaging the U.S. from Iraq and Afghanistan, and from other illegal and immoral wars.

· FIVE ·

Challenging Racism

U.S. SOLDIERS WHO FOUGHT IN VIETNAM were trained to think of the North Vietnamese people as "gooks." The objectification of the nonwhite enemy made it more palatable to kill and abuse them. American troops and mercenaries in Iraq likewise objectified their Iraqi prisoners when they sexually abused and sadistically humiliated them at the Abu Ghraib prison near Baghdad. One U.S. official, who told the *Los Angeles Times* that 50–100 Iraqis died in U.S. custody in 2003, said, "There was a mentality that the people we're in charge of are not humans."[1] Racism of this sort underlies and exacerbates a serious problem of racial prejudice within the military.

Today, as during the Vietnam War and before, racial discrimination, bigotry, and racial violence exist throughout the armed services, despite claims of equal opportunity. Although African Americans and other minority service members have made great strides in challenging and reducing discrimination, commands remain resistant to real equality, often ignoring or circumventing their regulations to do so. Conscious use of racism against an "enemy" encourages this internal racism and keeps it embedded in military culture.

This chapter examines the concrete ways in which racism has

been used to train and motivate soldiers to fight enemies whom they are taught to view as less than human—not just combatants but the population as a whole—and it scrutinizes the broader racism that has long plagued the military. We first consider the use of anti-Arab racism in training and in Iraq as exemplified by the testimony of one Army reservist during the 2008 Winter Soldier Investigation. We trace other examples of this dehumanization of the enemy and then equally troubling examples of racism against minority service members, including Arab American GIs. The chapter also details the remarkable development of GI antiracist movements during the Vietnam War, particularly the black power movement, and the ways in which many American soldiers came to understand the relationship between domestic racism and racism directed at the enemy.

In response to those antiracist movements, the military was forced to develop equal opportunity programs and regulations, which remain important today. Along with the broader GI antiwar movement, the black power movement demanded and legitimized many of the rights used by today's growing GI movement. We end the chapter with a discussion of the current regulations prohibiting racial discrimination and hate crimes, and practical ways to use those regulations.

Dehumanizing the Nonwhite Enemy Today

Mike Prysner enlisted in the Army Reserve in 2001 and served in Iraq between 2003 and 2004, assigned to the 10th Mountain Division, 173rd Airborne Brigade, as an aerial intelligence specialist. During the Winter Soldier hearings, he testified about his experiences in training and in the field, and their effect on him.

Prysner recounted that in his early training soldiers were told the Equal Opportunity Program had eliminated racism in the military. Yet after 9/11 new expressions became part of their training, terms like *camel jockey, raghead*, and *sand nigger*. This language originated not from fellow trainees, he explained, but from their sergeants, first sergeants, and even the battalion commander.

When he was sent to northern Iraq in 2003, Prysner testified, "I learned a new word, 'haji.' Haji was the enemy. Haji was every Iraqi. He was not a person, a father, a teacher, a worker." Prysner pointed out the irony of this derogatory term, because in Arabic *haji* is a respected word for Muslims who have made a sacred pilgrimage to Mecca, "in traditional Islam, the highest calling in the religion."[2] Yet the term of respect became a way of dehumanizing an entire people.

Prysner described one operation in which his unit forcibly removed Iraqi families from their homes without warning, explanation, or compensation, literally throwing people out into the streets. If the men of the household objected, they were detained and imprisoned.[3]

Later, assigned to work as an interrogator, Prysner observed physical and psychological abuse of hundreds of detainees. During one session, when he allowed a beaten and bleeding detainee to sit rather than stand as ordered, Prysner realized he was not protecting his own people against combatants but was protecting a detainee from the soldiers.[4]

Reflecting on these experiences, Prysner added, "I tried hard to be proud of my service, but all I could feel was shame. Racism could no longer mask the reality of the occupation. These are human beings. I've since been plagued by guilt."[5]

"Racism is a vital weapon deployed by this government," Prysner said. "It is a more important weapon than a rifle, a tank, a bomber, or a battleship. It is more destructive than an artillery shell, or a bunker buster, or a tomahawk missile ... Without racism soldiers would realize that they have more in common with the Iraqi people than they do with the billionaires who send us to war."[6]

Prysner's experience is by no means unique. Michael Blake, who served in Iraq from April 2003 to March 2004, reported that U.S. soldiers were told very little about Iraq, Iraqis, or Islam before arriving there. They were given a book of Arabic phrases, and, he said, "the message was always: 'Islam is evil' and 'They hate us.' Most of the guys I was with believed it."[7]

Geoff Millard, the Washington, DC chapter president of Iraq Veterans Against the War, testified at Winter Soldier that it's no surprise to hear anyone who has been deployed since 9/11 use the word *haji* to dehumanize not just people from Iraq and Afghanistan but also "anyone there who is not us." That included Pakistani KBR (formerly Kellogg Brown and Root) employees who did the laundry and worked inside the chow halls. "Everyone not in the U.S. force became a haji, not a person, not a name, a haji. I used to have conversations with members of my unit," Millard said, "and I would ask them why they use that term, especially members of my unit who are people of color. It used to shock me that they would. Their answers were very similar, almost always, 'They're just hajis. Who cares?'"[8]

Likewise, the word *raghead* is often used to portray Iraqis and Afghanis who wear turbans. Former corporal Stephen Funk related the practice of another former Marine corporal who trained his troops to operate machine guns by squeezing the trigger only as long as it took to chant, "Die, fucking raghead, die." At night, the squad leader would yell, "Let's go burn some turbans!"[9] Other pejorative terms included *towel head*, *camel jockey*, *jihad Johnny*, and *sand nigger*.

Drill sergeants at Fort Knox, Kentucky, would motivate their soldiers by reminding them of the 9/11 attacks and telling them they might have a chance to "kill us some towelheads." Aidan Delgado—who is Latino and knows Arabic—wrote, "It's a little shocking at first to have three hundred people chanting racist tunes, but gradually it fades into the background and you just do it . . . forgetting about what you're actually saying. I've certainly done it, and I can say with confidence that probably every soldier since September 11 has done the same in one form or another. It's part of the training." Delgado's commander warned his troops not to use racial epithets when the press was around. "Now, there's going to be media over there," he said, "so I don't want you to go telling them how you're going to go over there and kill some ragheads and burn some turbans." Delgado reported that the use of *haji* is "the ultimate form of subtle racism: becoming so ubiquitous that people forget it's a slur."[10]

Camilo Mejía found the "racist attitude toward cultural differences" to be common throughout his deployment in the Middle East. He quoted an old Iraqi man who once asked "why Americans treat Iraqis like dogs."[11]

Jody Casey pointed out that the disregard for Iraqis comes from the top. "They basically jam into your head: 'This is haji! This is haji!' You totally take the human being out of it and make them into a video game," he said. "If you start looking at them as humans, and stuff like that, then how are you going to kill them?"[12]

A number of Arab American soldiers and sailors have been singled out in training by drill instructors who used them as examples of what the enemy looks like. They were Arab; the enemy was Arab; Arab meant stupid, dirty, devious fanatics, ultimately less than human. Needless to say, the racist slurs and harassment encouraged in combat training followed these soldiers to the field. Military counseling groups find that Arab American GIs who come to them for help with complaints or discharges are often responding to a steady stream of such racism. Their experiences highlight an underlying reason for the strength of military racism today.

Dehumanizing Nonwhite Soldiers

During a January 2006 naval deployment in support of Operation Iraqi Freedom, a white junior petty officer in the company of other petty officers dangled a hangman's noose in front of African American sailor Jonathan Hutto's face. This appalling symbol of the mass lynchings of blacks was meant as a joke, but Hutto didn't think it was funny. As he later wrote in *Antiwar Soldier: How to Dissent within the Ranks of the Military,* Hutto sent a memo to his entire departmental chain of command and organized support from his shipmates.[13] The complaint resulted in an investigation and reduction in rank and a letter of reprimand for the perpetrator.

Hutto's first experience with white racism came at apprentice school after boot camp. When asked why he joined the Navy, Hutto said that he thought of the military as the best affirmative action employer in the country. As a result of that response, he was targeted severely by his instructors. He also reported that a petty officer made frequent positive comments about the Ku Klux Klan and Adolf Hitler.

Camilo Mejía reported that during training in Jordan, a white executive officer took digital photographs of Puerto Rican and black personnel and then pinned them to silhouettes for target practice. The officer's only punishment was transfer to an administrative position. Mejía also documented differential treatment of white and Latino soldiers when they fired accidental shots that hit soldiers without injuring them. Two Latino noncommissioned officers were severely reprimanded, while a white soldier went unpunished.[14]

When Aimee Allison was at Army boot camp at Fort Jackson, South Carolina, she overheard a white drill sergeant tell a dark-skinned recruit, "You look like Kunta Kinte [a slave from the TV miniseries *Roots*]." The drill sergeant encouraged the other recruits to join in the joke and laugh, so they would not only manifest agreement with his racism but also separate a black woman as "other" than the unit. Sharing her experiences as one of the writers of *10 Excellent Reasons Not to Join the Military*, Allison noted that her drill sergeant would often ask, "Where are my Chinese at?" when assigning laundry duty. He said, "For some reason, they do it the best." The drill sergeant also mocked a Sudanese immigrant. While handing the man a dark-colored rifle, the officer would loudly say that members of the unit couldn't tell where the rifle ended and the man's hands began. Then, when preparing for a night-ops maneuver, the drill sergeant instructed his troops to blow a whistle if they got lost. "Except you," he said to the Sudanese recruit. "You just smile and we'll see you in the dark."[15]

In 2006 the Southern Poverty Law Center reported the infiltration of neo-Nazis and skinheads into the military. The center revealed the presence of racist networks and organizations on a number of bases; over 300 extremists were identified at Fort Lewis, Washington, alone, from 2005 to 2006. Yet this was more than a decade after a scandal in December 1995, when two members of a skinhead gang in the Army's 82nd Airborne Division at Fort Bragg murdered a randomly selected African American couple. The killers were eventually sentenced to life in prison, and 19 other members of the 82nd Airborne received less than honorable discharges for neo-Nazi gang activities. Although this incident sparked a major military investigation of extremism in the military, congressional hearings, and new regulations aimed at racist organizations, the center's report found that these groups were still active 10 years later.[16]

Racist groups have their own reasons for organizing within the military as they attempt to bolster the paramilitary activities of the ultraright. But these organizations could not survive or grow in the military if there were not an atmosphere of racism in which they could take root. This is not to say that GIs are by nature racist but rather that the military engenders attitudes of racism. Until the military stops its use of racism against the enemy and takes firm steps to prevent discrimination and racial violence, the Klan and similar organizations will continue to find a home there.

Dehumanizing the Vietnamese

Racism within the military was rampant during the Vietnam War. The armed forces had officially ended segregation in 1948. Although this was an important victory, de facto racism in duty assignments, advancement, punishments, and daily life continued, sometimes spurred by white commanders and soldiers who resented the change. Many black veterans of the 1950s speak of their military experience with great bitterness.

During the Vietnam era, young African American men were drafted in disproportionate numbers. Many of them lacked the economic and social resources necessary for deferments and exemptions from the draft, such as family physicians who could document long-standing medical conditions for 4-F exemptions and money for college to obtain student deferments. White draftees of working-class and poor backgrounds faced similar problems, but people of color bore the greatest burden. Recruiters targeted black communities heavily, promising careers and a better future. And for many young black men entangled in a racist criminal justice system, military enlistment was a court-approved alternative to prison.

Once in the military, African American GIs were commonly assigned the dirtiest and most dangerous jobs and disproportionately represented in combat troops on the front lines of the war. In February 1967 the *New York Times* reported that black soldiers were dying in far higher numbers than whites.[17] Racial harassment was generally tolerated and sometimes encouraged by commands. Vulgar racist slurs were a fact of life for black troops, as they were for Latino, Native American, and other minority service members. In addition, the Ku Klux Klan and other racist groups had followers and sometimes entire chapters on bases in the United States and overseas. Racial violence posed a tangible danger for black and other nonwhite troops, particularly if they "mouthed off" to white soldiers, ignored taboos against interracial dating and marriage, or went to white-identified clubs or dances.

Asian American GIs faced unique problems during the war. In boot camp and combat training, instructors frequently singled them out to show other recruits "what a gook looks like." Other members of training platoons were encouraged to join in, laughing at and harassing the "slant eyes" in their ranks. Instructors used targeted bullying and abuse as intentional methods of dehumanizing and objectifying the Vietnamese people, who were lumped together as "Viet Cong." As with Arab American soldiers today, this racism followed Asian American soldiers throughout their service.

Inspired and encouraged by the civil rights and black power movements at home, African American service members began to challenge racism and discrimination in growing numbers. Their movement is chronicled in a wonderful Web site on African American involvement in the Vietnam War, AAVW.org.[18] Spontaneous meetings and protests grew into more organized dissent among black troops in the United States, Germany, and Vietnam. Protests—some simple gatherings of black soldiers, some organized demonstrations, and some spontaneous militant actions labeled "riots" by commands, whether or not any physical violence occurred—were reported at many bases. It became clear that widespread racism would no longer be accepted as a fact of life. In 1969 Secretary of the Army Stanley R. Resor stated,

> Formerly [the Negro soldier] countered acts of racial discrimination with hard work and endurance. Today he is more likely to make his resentment known. He needs a commander who recognizes such slogans as "black is beautiful" as the expression of pride, comradeship and solidarity that it represents to most young Negroes. The commander must understand his men before he writes off the spirited ones, who may be potential leaders as troublemakers or militants.[19]

Black soldiers formed organizations like the Black Servicemen's Caucus in San Diego (later to expand to Long Beach and New Orleans) and Unsatisfied Black Soldiers in Germany. Some African American soldiers joined the Black Panther Party. Others worked with white soldiers in groups like the Movement for a Democratic Military, with chapters in Navy port cities and at Marine bases up and down the California coast. These organizations and other, less formal, networks of soldiers combined calls for an end to the war with demands to end racism.

At the same time, Latino and Native American GIs, equally frustrated by racism and the war, took heart from antiracist and antiwar protests in their communities at home. Latino GIs joined chapters of the Brown Berets and other Chicano rights organizations, and Native American GIs joined the American Indian

Movement. Demands for an end to racism increased. At a number of bases, Latinos supported and were supported by radical black soldiers and white troops.

Increasing visibility of black protests and growing awareness of the racism they challenged added a new perspective to antiwar sentiments throughout the military. African American soldiers in Vietnam and those returning home raised the slogan "No Vietnamese ever called me 'nigger.'" GI activists and their civilian supporters discussed the parallels between racist policies and practices in the United States and the racism of the war itself. The underground GI press printed letters and articles about the ways in which racism was used to dehumanize Vietnamese as the enemy during boot camp and infantry training. Both black and white soldiers talked and wrote about command attempts to exploit white racism and black-white tensions in the military to keep soldiers from focusing on what many GIs identified as the "real enemy"— the military and the U.S. government.

With growing support from white soldiers, whose own radicalism often started with the war, radical black GIs became an important presence within the military and a mounting concern to the Pentagon. Demonstrations grew more frequent and more visible, receiving attention from the civilian antiwar movement and the press. The morale and political sensibility of enlisted personnel shifted and gradually began to affect the conduct of the war. When black sailors on the USS *Constellation* protested racism and poor working conditions, they were joined by white sailors.

Initially, the military leadership reacted to this growing movement with outrage and made serious efforts to clamp down on what they saw as a revolution. Military officials claimed that a small number of black militants were inciting otherwise happy troops to violence by playing on unfounded fears and confusion about legitimate military policies. Racial disturbances at Camp

Lejeune in North Carolina were labeled "riots," as were simple, quiet complaints about incidents of bigotry.[20] The military exaggerated the situation to the point of hysteria. Black service members who merely sounded radical were sometimes punished and often harassed. Those suspected of participation in demonstrations—sometimes on the basis of being outspoken or sometimes simply by being nearby when a protest took place—received harsh punishment, including sentences of two or more years in prison and punitive (bad conduct or even dishonorable) discharges. Military stockades held increasing numbers of black GIs who identified themselves as political prisoners.

The widely publicized fragging case of Private Billy Dean Smith is an instructive example. Fragging originally referred to throwing a fragmentation grenade into someone's tent; over time the term became a more general expression of soldiers' anger and rebellion, not necessarily a reference to homicide. Smith was accused, by supervisors who said he was too outspoken about black power, of fragging a lieutenant in Vietnam. He was returned to the United States for a general court-martial. The prosecution relied on Smith's comments about racism and on evidence discredited early in the case. A grenade pin and gunpowder were found in the pocket of one of his jackets. But the pin did not match the grenade used in the attack; gunpowder was everywhere in combat areas and likely to be found on most men where Smith's unit was camped.

The Army used this case as an example of the danger posed by the black power movement, a claim that ran into some difficulty when Private Smith was acquitted handily, because many soldiers, both black and white, had rallied to his support. The court-martial was reported widely in the underground GI press, support committees formed at a number of bases, and the case became a symbol of military racism and repression.

As repressive measures proved ineffective and protests grew, the Department of Defense initiated minor reforms to ease tensions. Commands allowed junior enlisted personnel to air their grievances directly to their commanders through an open-door policy, authorized meetings to discuss morale issues, and occasionally formed enlisted men's councils. Some commanders heard and acted on complaints of overtly racist behavior or language. But few real changes were made, and, not surprisingly, protests among black and other minority GIs continued.

Some top officers, like Colonel Heinl, and some members of Congress decried the lack of discipline and the growth of policies they considered too tolerant or permissive. They felt that command-sponsored meetings of enlisted personnel and opportunities for lower enlisted personnel to speak personally with their commanders without prior approval by the chain of command were unnecessary and unmilitary.

Early in the 1970s, military leaders concluded that the ground forces in Vietnam were unreliable and the war was in crisis. This assessment was based in large part on antiracist and antiwar attitudes among combat troops, who were seen as undependable, unwilling to fight, and often in open rebellion. Faced with real military losses, the Pentagon shifted from its the emphasis on ground combat, which had characterized the war from its inception, to an air war. Navy and Air Force presence was expanded in Southeast Asia and extensive bombing campaigns began. For sailors, in particular, this meant extended WestPac (Western Pacific) cruises, which placed considerable stress on an aging Navy fleet.

African American sailors' already poor working conditions worsened. Even though everyone was affected, black and other minority sailors were usually assigned to work below decks, where they operated, maintained, and patched up engines and equipment that were outdated and long overdue for replacement. Conditions were not only miserable but dangerous. Workspaces were cramped, hot, and dirty, and equipment was in perilously poor shape. Shipboard fires and accidents became a growing problem. As they were forced into greater participation in the war, these sailors were reminded daily that their working conditions and treatment were racist and inhumane. Antiwar and antiracist protests in Navy towns and aboard ship increased dramatically.

In the fall of 1972, black sailors aboard the USS *Constellation* and USS *Kitty Hawk*, aircraft carriers homeported in San Diego, held protests against racism and dangerous shipboard conditions, and hundreds of sailors joined in those actions. Spontaneous protests and some planned ones—work stoppages, sit-ins, and other types—preceded and followed the *Kitty Hawk* and *Constellation* "riots," though these were the most widely reported. Official Navy reviews and congressional hearings on the two "riots" placed the blame solely on black sailors, refused to acknowledge the existence of racist practices, and in one case denied that the black sailors were even acting out of any belief that there were racist practices onboard. The idea that the sailors were protesting dangerous conditions or the war was outside the military's field of vision.

But the Congressional Black Caucus and civil rights groups knew better. Beginning in 1971, the caucus held widely reported hearings in which it interviewed black soldiers and sailors and cataloged discriminatory policies and practices as well as incidents of overt racism. Representatives Ron Dellums and John Conyers pressed for an overhaul in military policy. The National Association for the Advancement of Colored People (NAACP) sent investigators to bases in Germany, where they found both racism and extremist organizations such as the Ku Klux Klan. The NAACP, other civil rights organizations, and American Civil Liberties

Union (ACLU) received calls and letters from hundreds of black GIs, who asked for investigations and assistance.

In response to all of this, DoD finally developed regulations and programs designed to reduce racism and promote equal opportunity, an effort that grew into the Military Equal Opportunity Program (MEO or EO). The Pentagon established complaint procedures and training plans on discrimination, including discrimination based on nationality, ethnicity, or gender. The system developed in part from legitimate concerns about the extent of racism in the military but also from a hope that the black power movement would be defused. DoD's efforts were limited, and the results were mixed. They represented a real victory for African American and other minority service members, and did much to reduce overt and institutional forms of discrimination and bigotry. At the same time, many considered the programs too limited— African American GIs were rightly skeptical of efforts to placate them and encourage cooperation in an institution that continued racist practices at all levels.

Using the System to Fight Racism

The original EO program grew to include a strongly worded DoD directive and implementing service regulations that mandate a Military Equal Opportunity Program, prohibiting discrimination, establishing complaint procedures, and requiring education and training to reduce racism and other forms of discrimination.[21] Racial and other specified types of discrimination are prohibited in duty assignments, promotions, and other aspects of military life. Racist behavior, racially-motivated harassment, and overtly racist language are also proscribed, and "aggravated" racist acts are sometimes grounds for disciplinary action or misconduct discharge. In theory, regular training at all commands teaches GIs not to discriminate but to show respect for diversity.

EO complaint procedures vary from service to service, so GIs who want to file grievances are well advised to read the regulations and seek help from civilian attorneys or military counselors such as those listed in the Appendix. Ironically, the regulations encourage service members not to use EO complaints. All of them suggest that the best first step is to speak to the person against whom a complaint might be made—to politely ask the person making racist comments or dangling a noose to stop. The second suggested remedy is to speak to the complainant's immediate superior, unless, of course, that person is the problem. Thereafter, the regs suggest, aggrieved GIs should talk to each and every supervisor and officer in their immediate chain of command. The DoD directive explains that "the chain of command is the primary and preferred channel for identifying and correcting discriminatory practices." None of these steps are required, but complainants are often reprimanded for skipping one or more of them.

In addition to, or instead of, requests to the chain of command, EO regulations set out informal and formal EO complaint procedures. In most services these are first taken to a command-appointed EO officer (who is not necessarily of officer rank). Needless to say, informal complaints are encouraged, as these are simply verbal complaints handled informally and requiring little formal action or reporting. EO officers look into the problem and talk to the complainants' commanders, who may or may not take action.

However, soldiers have the right to make formal, written EO complaints, which must be investigated, "resolved," and reported to service headquarters. Many GIs and advocates consider this the only EO method that should be used, and they recommend outside assistance with every complaint.

In most of the services, soldiers bring their complaints to EO officers or write complaints with their help. Except in the Air Force, where EO officers conduct their own investigations, the EO officers turn complaints over to the complainants' immediate commanders for investigation, decision, and action, unless the commanders are implicated in the complaints. In those cases, EO officers take complaints to the next level of command. Commanders designate someone to investigate the complaint, often an officer in the command but sometimes a local inspector general (IG). In the Air Force, EO officers handle much of the investigation.

Advocates in this area note that GIs lose all control over complaints once they are made. Although GIs are entitled to reports about the investigation, they are seldom given details and are not always told what, if any, punishment or corrective action is taken. Investigating officers may or may not choose to interview the complainants and all of the witnesses they name, and are not required to use the complainants' suggestions or documentation. Investigations often conclude that the racist incident did not occur, that the GI who complained was at fault, and that little or no discrimination was involved. At times, investigators agree that an act of discrimination actually took place, but find that it was insignificant.

Generally, investigating officers (or, in the Air Force, EO officers) report their results to the appointing commanders. Complainants' commanding officers then determine the legitimacy of complaints and make decisions on their resolution. Complainants may appeal to higher authority if they are not satisfied with the results and may ultimately take their appeal to the office of the secretary of the service.

These complaints have some value. Honest commands may use them to remedy problems, the military must keep records of the results, and EO complaints provide documentation and a paper trail for complainants who must appeal, make another type of complaint, or take the matter to court. EO complaints demonstrate that GIs have done everything according to approved procedure and, as courts frequently require, have exhausted all of their administrative remedies.

But EO complaints and less formal requests to the command have drawbacks as well. Service members who complain about racism (or other discrimination or misconduct) often face retaliation. This may involve harassment from the person complained about and his or her friends, or disciplinary and administrative actions from the command, actions allegedly unrelated to the complaint but that happen to coincide with it. Fortunately, the Military Whistleblower Protection Act, discussed in Chapter 4, can be used against such retaliation.

Because the EO system is weak, many service members use other complaint procedures in addition to or instead of EO complaints. One common approach is a complaint under Article 138 of the UCMJ, the redress of grievance complaint, also discussed in Chapter 4. Other alternatives include formal meetings with commanders, sometimes with an attorney present; complaints to the service or DoD inspector general (IG); requests for help to members of Congress; or creative complaints under no particular authority, submitted by an attorney or other advocate to higher levels of command. In addition, complainants who feel the system has failed them may speak to civil rights organizations or the media or file suit in federal court. In all of these procedures, outside legal assistance can be of great value.

Complaints against racism are neither user-friendly nor entirely safe. But they offer an important way to challenge and document military racism. Although complaints through proper channels lack the impact of collective actions such as petitions or demonstrations, they are still valuable. The history of the Vietnam-era movement shows that organizing and protest by African American, Latino, and other minority GIs, supported by other service members, offer the greatest chance of achieving real change.

Many of the soldiers who testified at Winter Soldier 2008 discussed the pervasiveness of racist behavior, often admitting they had used racial epithets and engaged in brutality that dehumanized Iraqis and Afghanis. Their statements demonstrate that racism harms those who use it as well as the victims. The GIs who testified, and other soldiers and veterans, point out the links between racism and dehumanization of the enemy and ongoing domestic military racism. It is incumbent upon the service members to resist the racist modeling of their superiors and challenge racist behaviors against minority troops. Objection to one form of racism inherently challenges the other as well. Through the military's complaint procedures, public exposure of this racism, and protests by minority and white soldiers alike, both problems can be addressed.

· SIX ·

Sexual Harassment and Sexual Assault in the Military

SEXISM AND SEXUAL IMAGERY are used in military training in much the same way that racism is. Young soldiers are encouraged to think of strength and discipline in combat as sexual prowess; to equate military violence and sexual violence; to see disobedience, nonconformity, or weakness as feminine. Soldiers who cannot or will not perform as expected are told they are women or "faggots." Such training methods become necessary when soldiers are not inspired by a patriotic cause but are confronted with an illegal and immoral war they have no desire to fight.

Sexual discrimination in the military, like racism, has a life and tradition of its own, with roots preceding its extensive use in training. But sexual discrimination in training, first used extensively during the Vietnam War, has so exacerbated the underlying sexism that it is now deeply embedded in military culture. Despite Department of Defense claims that the military is an equal opportunity employer, women soldiers experience discrimination in training, duty assignments, promotions, and many other areas. Exclusion from direct combat roles is only a small part of the picture, for female GIs encounter gender-based assumptions about their worth as soldiers and their abilities, strength, intelligence, and honor. For many servicewomen, however, sexual harassment and sexual assault pose a far more serious problem than discriminatory practices.

The military defines sexual harassment as a form of sexual discrimination involving unwelcome sexual advances, requests for sexual favors, or other conduct of a sexual nature, particularly when the harasser says or implies that refusal will harm the victim's military career, or when the behavior creates a hostile work environment. Sexual assault, including rape and other forcible or unwanted sexual contact, is considered separate from discrimination.

The dangers of sexual harassment and rape have become basic facts of military life. Servicewomen run a much higher risk of assault than do their civilian counterparts, and the danger comes from male colleagues and superiors. Sexual harassment is endemic in the workplace and in all aspects of life on bases and ships. The Pentagon has been forced to admit that it has a climate of sexual harassment that fosters a high rate of sexual assaults.

This chapter examines the experience of one young soldier who was sexually assaulted and harassed by superiors within her command in Kuwait, in Iraq, and at her station in the United States. We consider specific examples of harassment and violence against military women and the shocking statistics revealed by independent reports and the military's own studies. We review the sordid history of sexual harassment and assault in the military during Vietnam, when the military began extensive use of sexism in training, and since then. Finally, we scrutinize the official complaint mechanisms offered by the military and alternatives that may provide better results.

Military Sexual Assault:
One Soldier's Story

While stationed with the Army in the Persian Gulf, Specialist Suzanne Swift was sexually harassed repeatedly by noncommissioned officers. She made a complaint against a sergeant in 2005. Although the incident was substantiated by the command, the man received only a letter of reprimand and transfer to another base. In Iraq Swift's direct supervisor coerced her to engage in sex over a period of several months on threat of disciplinary action. After her return to the States, Swift faced further harassment at Fort Lewis, Washington, including an "order" to report to a sergeant's bed. Complaints to her command led only to bullying and other harassment. Facing a second deployment to Iraq with one of her original harassers, Swift went AWOL in January 2006, two days before her unit was scheduled to leave.

Swift was arrested six months later at her mother's home and returned to Fort Lewis. There, she told military officials about her experiences, and they promised to look into the matter. Despite her complaints and a civilian psychiatrist's report that Swift suffered from post-traumatic stress disorder, the command charged her for going AWOL and missing the deployment. Army officials later decided that Swift's complaints against two superiors lacked merit.

In December Swift was tried by a summary court-martial, the lowest form of military court. She was sentenced to 30 days confinement and a reduction in rank by one pay grade. Even with time off for good behavior, Swift was forced to spend Christmas in military confinement. She was later transferred to another base and told that she could serve out the remainder of her enlistment instead of receiving a bad discharge. Swift's experiences are chronicled on a Web site set up by supporters, SuzanneSwift.org.

Susanne Swift's story of sexual assault is only one of many. The problem of sexual assault in combat areas has been verified by many others, including Colonel Janis Karpinski, the former commander of Abu Ghraib prison. Karpinski is one of the highest-ranking women to speak out about the problem of rape and sexual assault among Army soldiers in Iraq. "It was out of control," Karpinski told a group of students at San Diego's Thomas Jefferson School of Law in October 2005. She explained that GIs were given a military 800 number that women could use to report sexual assaults. But they often had no phone, and no one answered that number, which was based in the United States—women who reached it got a recorded message. Even after more than 83 incidents were reported during a six-month period in Iraq and Kuwait, Karpinski added, the 24-hour rape hotline was still answered by a machine that told callers to leave a message.

Karpinski testified at the International Commission of Inquiry on Crimes against Humanity Committed by the Bush Administration in New York in January 2006. In a startling revelation, she stated that several women at Camp Victory in Iraq had died of dehydration because they refused to drink liquids late in the day. The women were afraid of being raped by male soldiers if they had to walk to the women's latrine after dark. Karpinski also stated that Lt. Gen. Ricardo Sanchez, the former senior U.S. military commander in Iraq, gave orders to cover up the cause of death for some of these women. Karpinski explained that a military surgeon had mentioned such deaths in a briefing to superiors in Iraq: "And rather than make everybody aware of that—because that's shocking, and as a leader if that's not shocking to you then you're not much of a leader—what they told the surgeon to do is don't brief those details anymore. And don't say specifically that they're women. You can provide that in a written report, but don't brief it in the open anymore." The surgeon was also told not to list dehydration as a cause of death.[1]

Periodically, exposés or scandals reveal shocking incidents of sexual harassment or sexual assault in the military, sometimes in unexpected settings, sometimes by high-ranking officers, sometimes involving very young women just entering the military. Many entail extreme violence and a remarkable degree of crudeness.

Each time, women have come forward, usually after unsuccessful attempts to complain through military channels, and told the media or members of Congress about the incidents. They have reported rapes at the service academies; sexual assaults and harassment in workplaces, barracks, and aboard ships; and sexual assaults in combat areas. Each time, publicity about their reports leads other women—other cadets at academies, young women in training, and other GIs in combat areas—in the same situation to file complaints. Each scandal has led to congressional inquiries or hearings and military or independent studies. Each round of reports and congressional findings forces DoD to issue new regulations prohibiting and punishing misconduct, and new training programs to prevent it. And each time, follow-up investigations have shown not only that the problems continue, but that women who use new regulations to report misconduct face reprisals and harassment by their commands. The numbers are staggering. In March 2008 the Pentagon office responsible for tracking sexual assault cases announced 2,688 reported cases of sexual assault in the military during fiscal year 2007. Of those, only about 600 resulted in some sort of action against the assailant. And of that number, only one-third went to courts-martial, another one-third received lower-level nonjudicial punishment, and the final one-third received involuntary discharge or administrative action.[2]

But those figures were called into question when the Government

Accountability Office told a House of Representatives subcommittee that it found sexual assaults were significantly underreported in the military.[3] GAO's own surveys and a Department of Defense gender relations survey in 2006 showed that more than half of those who were assaulted declined to report the assault. These findings were consistent with media reports that most women did not complain after rapes or assaults, usually fearing that nothing would be done or that their complaints would lead to reprisals and damage their careers.[4]

Figures on sexual harassment are similarly shocking. A 2005 survey found that 60 percent of women who served in the reserves or National Guard have been harassed, though less than one-fourth of them reported the harassment.[5] Although military and civilian reports and surveys differ, most conclude that at least one-third and more likely over half of all women in the military have experienced some form of harassment by fellow service members or superiors. Appalling as these figures are, they hardly portray the horror of individual rapes and assaults.

Military Sexual Assault: The History

During the Vietnam War, women made up only two percent of the armed forces and served in only a few noncombat positions.[6] Women worked primarily as nurses and medical assistants, and a few served as clerical personnel. Although banned from combat, many women were stationed in Vietnam. Little public discussion of sexual harassment and rape, let alone sexual discrimination, took place.

Few military women participated in visible antiwar protests in the Vietnam era. This fact reflected not only women's numbers in the military but also the low level of attention given to them by the GI movement and the lack of recognition of the special issues they faced. Only a handful of women were prominent, among them Susan Schnall, a Navy nurse who was court-martialed for releasing antiwar flyers from an airplane over military bases in the San Francisco Bay Area in 1968. But, more quietly, female GIs wrote for underground papers and, together with civilian women, were involved in some coffeehouses and antiwar centers.

Toward the end of the war, the GI movement, along with the broader civilian antiwar and feminist movements, began to talk about sexism and sexual harassment in the military. GI newspapers carried letters and articles discussing the ways in which drill instructors, training manuals, and unit leaders in the field used sexual imagery and degradation of women to train and motivate troops. David Cortright recounted his own observations of the use of sexual imagery in military training: "Machismo, the attitude of assertive male superiority, is an essential element of military culture and plays a key role in conditioning hostility and insensitivity among servicemen." Describing phallic allusions in weapons training, Cortright concluded that "the discrimination encountered by servicewomen seems rooted in sexist prejudices at the very foundation of military life."[7] Discussion of the problems women faced in the military generally focused on institutional discrimination; any mention of sexual harassment and rape was rare. As the war wound down, however, antiwar activists, military counselors, and women's organizations began to pay more attention to both discrimination and harassment. In 1971 the National Organization for Women (NOW) adopted a policy resolution condemning the degradation of women by sexist practices in the military.

In 1972 a short article titled "Little-Known Program: Equal Opportunity Must Be Accorded Women" ran in the *Commander's Digest*. It explained that the Equal Opportunity programs established to deal with racial discrimination also included provisions "removing any irrelevancy such as sex from consideration in the total work environment." The article quoted Assistant Secretary of the Army Hadlai Hull, who told civilian Army personnel, "Clearly, women are being under-utilized in the Army, and this under-utilization is due in part to sex discrimination."[8]

Some years after the war was over the true magnitude of the problem came to light, as the VA began to see large numbers of women with unique stress disorders. Particular credit goes to women in the VA—psychologists, counselors, and doctors—who pressed for recognition of military sexual trauma and the development of special treatment centers for the women traumatized by rape or assault in the service. Columbia School of Journalism professor Helen Benedict described the problems of rape, sexual assault, and harassment as severe and extensive during the Vietnam War.[9]

The problem grew almost exponentially after the war as the military started recruiting more women due to the end of the draft and shrinking enlistment pools. In 1972 DoD developed specific plans to increase the use of women. Women were admitted into a number of traditionally male military occupational specialties during the 1970s and thereafter. By mid-1977, the Army, Navy, and Air Force had each doubled their numbers of female personnel, and the Marine Corps had increased participation by 40 percent. By 1979 women made up 10 percent of military personnel.

Although the Pentagon viewed this expansion as a way to free up the available male recruits for more-important combat roles, many male officers and enlisted men deeply resented the incursion into their territory. As traditionally male military occupational specialties were gradually opened to women, some men complained. Their complaints were leveled for the practical reason that men were less likely to serve in "comfortable" assignments and to have coveted shore billets or relatively pleasant rear-guard jobs, which were now increasingly filled by women.

On a more fundamental level, many service men felt threatened personally and sexually by the fact that women were performing traditionally male jobs just as well as, and in some cases better than, their male counterparts. The idea of taking orders from women heightened the problem for some men. Common military wisdom at the time was that women enlisted for one of two reasons—to find a man or to find a woman. Female enlisted personnel and officers were, and sometimes still are, presumed to be promiscuous or lesbian.

But the problem of sexual harassment was not officially recognized until 1979, and the services announced zero tolerance programs in the early 1980s. The Defense Department Advisory Committee on Women in the Services (DACOWITS) found sexual harassment to be a major problem at overseas bases in 1986, and its findings helped to spark congressional hearings in 1987 and 1988. The first DoD directives dealing specifically with sexual harassment were finally published in 1988. In 1989 the Pentagon started to keep statistics of harassment cases that were reported all the way to headquarters.

Then came the Navy's Tailhook scandal, one of the first public exposés of sexual harassment and misconduct in the military. The Tailhook Association, an unofficial organization of Navy fighter pilots, held its annual convention in Las Vegas in September 1991. The convention actually included seminars on aviation, but Tailhook conventions were notorious for their wild parties and drunken carousing. That year, male pilots apparently outdid themselves, harassing and assaulting a number of women, including other Navy officers and civilians staying at the convention hotel.

Women were groped and fondled in the hallways. Some, including Lt. Paula Coughlin, were forced to run a "gauntlet" of drunken men who grabbed and screamed at them. In a hospitality suite, women were invited to drink beer from a tap mounted on the wall—a plastic rhinoceros whose penis dispensed the beer.

Some of the women reported the assaults to their commands. When their complaints were met with silence, several of them spoke to their members of Congress or the press. Their accounts were corroborated by outraged civilian hotel guests. Only then did the Navy take any action. The Naval Investigative Service (NIS, now the Naval Criminal Investigative Service, or NCIS) sent agents to interview pilots and look into the allegations, but it reported that only minor improprieties had occurred at the conference.

Members of Congress, reporters, and the public were skeptical. Under pressure, DoD turned the matter over to its own Defense Investigative Service, which determined that the reports of assaults and outrageous misconduct were true and that Navy commands had tried to cover up the misconduct to protect their male pilots. Civilian press reports revealed that top Navy officials had been present at the conference. Although the Navy argued no evidence was found that the officials had participated, it admitted that they had done nothing to stop the misconduct. Ultimately, four admirals were relieved of their commands, the Secretary of the Navy resigned, and a few pilots eventually received minor punishment.

One result of the Tailhook scandal was an inquiry by the House Armed Services Committee. Among other things the committee looked at the need to change military culture to address the problem of assaults. It compared sexual harassment in the military to military racism, spoke glowingly of the development of equal opportunity programs, and suggested that, as with racial discrimination, harassment could be overcome through military "leadership commitment, career-long mandatory sexual harassment awareness training, [and] clear demonstration through disciplinary action and career impact that certain behaviors will not be tolerated."[10] None of these things happened.

Reports of rape and sexual assault from the first Gulf war, where military women were isolated from civilian legal and social support, appeared not long after the war. Rape reports in Kuwait and Bahrain came to the attention of the media and Congress, shocking many who had assumed that wartime discipline and cohesion would protect women from the men serving next to them. Thereafter, the pattern of scandals continued, including the rape of new recruits at Aberdeen Proving Ground and assaults at the prestigious service academies, more reports and regs, and little substantive change.

Training Soldiers: Power, Violence, and Sex

The Department of Defense periodically tries to identify the underlying causes of the high numbers of assault and harassment cases in the services. In reality the studies usually identify other symptoms rather than causes. Failure or refusal to examine the basic reasons for a culture that not only tolerates but sometimes encourages harassment and assault prevents the military from addressing those reasons. As a result, DoD's plans for improvement have largely been cosmetic and unsuccessful.

DoD has identified such causes as lack of clarity about policy, failure to train soldiers to understand what sexual harassment is, and paucity of follow-up training in prevention and response. Despite the requirement of repeated trainings, including predeployment briefings, military officials continue to say that male soldiers don't understand the definitions and often harass out of ignorance. The military has long provided materials for GI training programs and information on what harassment entails, with specific definitions and examples—but these are often not used at local commands. Studies make general reference to a culture that tolerates sexual harassment and a poor "command climate" on these issues.

The military has cited alcohol and party culture as contributing factors to continued sexual harassment, along with the pressures of working in close quarters with women (read: women being allowed to serve in traditionally male jobs) and societal problems. The military's early claims that recruits simply brought sexist attitudes and behaviors with them from the civilian world, or more recent assertions that lowered enlistment standards cause higher incidents of misconduct, have been hard to sustain. They fly in the face of the large disparity between civilian and military assault figures and the reports of a much higher incidence of rape in communities located adjacent to military bases than in other, civilian, areas. Some, but not many, military reports acknowledge that military sexual harassment provides a favorable climate for sexual assault, as congressional reports and critics have been saying for some years.

But the military has never addressed the underlying causes of sexual harassment and assault, and it cannot do so unless it accepts fundamental criticism of the way it has come to train and sustain its forces. At the heart of these problems is the fact that sexual harassment and assault result in large part from the intentional use of sexism—sexual imagery and sexual brutality—in military indoctrination and training.

During basic training male soldiers are taught to equate manliness and sexual prowess with proficiency as a warrior; sexual violence with military violence; and disobedience or nonconformity with weakness, femininity, and negatively portrayed homosexuality. Drill instructors use crude parallels between recruits' rifles and penises when discussing maintenance and use of weapons, and they emphasize violent sexual imagery in combat training. This use of sexual violence is routine, showing up in everything from marching chants to motivational taunts.

Such training, like the conscious use of racial stereotypes and names, encourages objectification of and brutality toward a perceived enemy. The training creates soldiers who obey orders without thinking as many are conditioned to engage in the most heinous violence. Indoctrination of this sort is reinforced in military culture, in the sexist banter and violent imagery common at most commands, in the use of sexual gratification as a reward for good soldiering in ports of call after long deployments and in rest and recuperation (R&R) after periods of combat. Sexism and sexual harassment become male bonding mechanisms within military units, used to maintain camaraderie and morale. Inevitably, command tolerance of and participation in harassment prevents enforcement of regulations and protects those accused of harassment or assault. When soldiers cannot be motivated by patriotism and the belief that they are fighting for a just cause, other basic motivating concepts must be found to replace them. Sexism, racism, and homophobia are coldly and manipulatively used to get soldiers to fight.

Response to Sexual Assault: More Hearings, Studies, and Regulations

One of the most recent studies of sexual assault in the military was released in 2004. At congressional insistence, Secretary of Defense Donald Rumsfeld directed the under secretary of defense for personnel and readiness to undertake a 90-day review of sexual assault policies. "Sexual assault will not be tolerated in the Department of Defense," Rumsfeld declared. [11]

In response the DoD published a 99-page report by a DoD task force on sexual assault in April 2004 on care for sexual assault victims.[12] It affirmed, "The chain of command is responsible for ensuring that policies and practices regarding crime prevention and security are in place for the safety of service members." The rates of reported alleged sexual assault were 69.1 and 70.0 per 100,000 uniformed service members in 2002 and 2003. Yet because of substantial differences in the definition of sexual assault, those rates were not directly comparable to rates reported by civilian agencies. The report found that assault remained widespread, that women were afraid to report assaults, and that they were unofficially discouraged from doing so. Like other recent congressional hearings and media reports, it emphasized the lack of confidentiality as a major problem.

Notably, the report concluded that low sociocultural status (i.e., age, education, race/ethnicity, marital status) and low organizational status (i.e., pay grade and years of active duty service) were associated with an increased likelihood of both sexual assault and sexual harassment.

Despite this and other studies, new training programs, and new regulations, little has changed. As the numbers mentioned earlier in this chapter show, DoD has made no real progress in eliminating or reducing the number of assaults. Reports of rape and other assaults at the service academies, in combat areas, among recruiters, and in basic training demonstrate simply more of the same. Despite the current regulations on sexual assault mandated by Congress, along with intensified training on sexual assault policy and more detailed record keeping of reported assaults, the military environment is no safer for women.

Retaliation for Sexual Assault Complaints

The scandal lies not just in the continuing pattern of harassment and assault but also in the military's shameful response. As the Pentagon's own studies conclude, women who report assault or harassment—called "complainants" in harassment cases—are very often ignored, threatened, and labeled troublemakers or lesbians, though usually not in such polite terms. Women who make complaints have no right to demand that coworkers or supervisors who harass or assault them be moved elsewhere. Thus women may face further harassment from offenders and offenders' friends. Beyond that, hostile commands frequently retaliate against complainants with threats of charges for making false statements, poor performance evaluations, disciplinary action, unwanted and unnecessary psychiatric evaluations, and involuntary discharges. Reporting sexual harassment or rape is regarded by many women as a "career buster." To make matters worse, military medical protocols and investigative agency guidelines lag far behind civilian standards. According to an important series on military sexual assault in the *Denver Post*, women raped in combat zones repeatedly report poor medical treatment, lack of counseling, failure to gather forensic evidence and other evidence, incomplete criminal investigations, threats of punishment after making complaints, and a disrespect for their safety.[13]

As a result, many women who experience assault or harassment choose to hide their attacks. Among those who do complain, many give up on the process when it stalls. Some women go AWOL for their own safety or from the stress of the assault, as Susanne Swift did.

Using the System to Fight Sexual Assault

Dissatisfied with DoD's efforts in 2004, and angered with new reports on an ongoing sexual assault scandal at the Air Force Academy in Colorado, Congress mandated a new policy and new regulations on sexual assault in the National Defense Authorization Act of 2005. The Pentagon responded with a series of brief "directive-type memoranda" from Under Secretary of Defense for Personnel and Readiness David Chu; these memoranda were later turned into the current regulations: Department of Defense Instruction 6459.02, Department of Defense Directive 6459.01, and parallel service regulations.[14]

The regs emphasize that sexual assault is a detriment to military readiness, that education about sexual assault policy needs to be increased and regularly repeated at all command levels, and that improvements in response to sexual assaults are necessary to make victims more willing to report them. The regulations do not address sexual harassment or revise existing regulations on that problem. DoD's analysis of sexual assault remains shallow, the links to sexual harassment and sexism in military culture are simply ignored, and the underlying significance of sexual objectification and sexual violence in training and motivation is still unquestioned.

The DoD directive and instruction and implementing service regulations include some improvements over previous regulations on assault, but problems remain. Confidentiality is supposed to be the linchpin of the new policy on sexual assault (but not sexual harassment). For the first time, women may make "restricted" (confidential) reports in which their privacy is protected, but the assaulter is not investigated. Under a new sexual assault prevention and response program, each branch of the service is required to appoint sexual assault response coordinators (SARCs) and victims' advocates at every major command, including those in combat areas. These personnel are supposed to provide immediate assistance on a 24/7 basis to women who report assaults, to ensure that victims receive emergency medical care if they need or desire it, and to help victims in negotiating the sexual assault reporting procedures. SARCs have an obligation to track reported cases until they are "resolved," oversee what is supposed to be extensive sexual assault prevention training, and maintain statistical information. Health providers, law enforcement, victims' advocates, and other "first responders" are to receive training in the policy and its limited victims' rights.

Servicewomen who report assaults to military medical personnel, SARCs, or victims' advocates can request that the entire case be kept restricted to medical personnel, advocates (if wanted), SARCs, and perhaps chaplains. In theory not even the soldier's commanding officer will be told of the assault, though a number of exceptions limit this confidentiality, and all confidentiality is lost if the GI tells others. Restricted reporting is not intended to place any limits on victims' access to medical care and counseling.

But the regulations say that SARCs and advocates should encourage women to use the unrestricted (nonconfidential) reporting method, though in theory they will not pressure victims to do so. Some women choose to make restricted reports initially so that they can take time to consider their options before subjecting themselves to the often-traumatic experience of an investigation and trial. Soldiers may switch from a restricted to an unrestricted report within a year, though unrestricted reports cannot later be made confidential.

Unrestricted reports allow investigation and prosecution of the offenders. They can be made to any military personnel, who must then inform the SARC; commanders are quickly notified as well. Investigators and military law enforcement personnel who may handle assault cases are to receive training about their role under the policy. They are required to treat GIs who report rape or other assaults with dignity and respect, and to avoid subjecting them to "revictimization" with unnecessarily repetitious or humiliating questions, and in some cases they actually do so. If the GIs wish, advocates will accompany them to all interviews, appointments, and court hearings. Their role is to ensure that victims receive medical and other assistance and understand the policy and procedures, and to provide support through the process, but they don't actually advocate on the soldiers' behalf.

The regulations state that retaliation for sexual assault complaints is improper, but they do not add new remedies for reprisals. Those who complain have some protection under the Military Whistleblowers Protection Act, discussed in Chapter 4, although many servicewomen feel its effectiveness is limited. The policy contains a slight improvement over previous policies in that it has a provision allowing commanding officers, at their own discretion, to delay punishment for any collateral misconduct, such as illegal drinking, by the victim. No suggestion is made that such collateral misconduct be excused, or punishment limited, to encourage women to report assaults in those circumstances.

And, of course, decisions about whether complaints are credible and misconduct occurred are made by commanders, who also decide whether assaulters will be punished, administratively discharged, or merely reprimanded. GIs who report assaults still face command disbelief, illegal efforts to protect the assaulters, and informal harassment from assaulters, assaulters' friends, or the command itself.

Attorneys and military counselors always urge that women who are considering or have made reports become familiar with the regulations, document their cases carefully, not rely entirely on investigators' work, and if at all possible involve a civilian legal advocate as early as possible. Because an assault and the pressure of command response can prove extremely stressful, outside support through civilian rape crisis centers and women's groups is also important. Used carefully and somewhat defensively, the regulations can be a valuable tool in responding to assaults and preventing further assaults. In addition to the other organizations listed in the Resources in the Appendix of this book, the Miles Foundation (at 203-270-7861) has proven an invaluable resource, providing legal and emotional support to servicewomen while working to improve the military's policy. The Service Women's Action Network (SWAN, at www.servicewomen.org), is a new organizing and support project focused on active duty and veteran women, particularly women of color.

Sexual harassment cases are handled under entirely separate equal opportunity (EO) regulations and procedures, which are discussed in Chapter 5. Just as with those harmed by racial discrimination, victims of sexual harassment may decide to use other complaint procedures in addition to or instead of EO complaints. EO officers generally make only recommendations and suggestions to the command, and commanders decide what, if anything, will be done in response to harassment. On the other hand, complaints under Article 138 of the UCMJ, congressional inquiries, and informal complaints made with the help of civilian attorneys or advocates—all discussed in Chapter 4—may give service members more control over the outcome. The GIs, rather than officials who may be the cause of the problem in the first place, decide whether the results are sufficient and whether complaints should be escalated.

Women who have made complaints of harassment or gone through investigations of assault frequently find that outside legal and emotional support are critical. One woman may have a hard time standing against the person who has assaulted or harassed her—particularly if he is a supervisor or commander—against all of his buddies, and against a hostile command. But one woman with a civilian advocate and a local women's group or rape crisis center standing with her will give the command pause and may change the outcome and impact of the complaint.

In the short run, no significant reduction in harassment and assault will occur unless military women are empowered to make real complaints, the complaints are handled with the respect and thoroughness other crime reports receive, and women are given real protection from their assaulters and from command retaliation. This requires continuing pressure on the military to enforce its regulations. It means demanding that victims receive legal assistance from military and civilian counsel from the moment they contemplate making a complaint. It must mean keeping pressure on Congress and the media to report those cases in which women want outside exposure, anonymously or otherwise. And it means that the women's movement and the antiwar movement must include this issue in their work, developing campaigns to support military women in cooperation with GI rights and counseling groups. In this way, servicewomen can demand justice in individual cases and, when they wish, use those cases to point to the underlying problems in the military.

In the long run, real change requires much more. As the GI antiwar movement and black power movement have shown, change often comes from pressure within the military. GIs—men and women alike—can stop individual acts of harassment and protect women from assault. GIs, veterans, and military families can challenge the use of sexism and sexual violence in training and the climate of harassment that dehumanizes women and encourages rape and assault, and they can end the "don't ask, don't tell" policy and challenge the homophobia on which it is based.

But significant change can take place only if the military is required to make basic changes in the ways that soldiers are trained and encouraged to fight. If it is not to prove manliness, if it is not a form of sexual dominance, the motivation for fighting must be honorable—protecting the weak against oppression and fighting for things this country and its people truly believe, rather than for symbols used by military and political leaders. It would mean a military in which discipline and obedience of orders would flow from commitment and belief in the cause, rather than from a desire to prove oneself as a man. And it would mean disengagement from illegal and immoral wars that soldiers and their families do not support.

· SEVEN ·

The Medical Side of War

THE MILITARY'S HEALTH CARE SYSTEM, perhaps more than any other sector of the armed forces, has been overwhelmed by the current wars. Pressed to maintain troop strength and readiness, commands give little attention to troops' medical problems and often actively discourage injured or ill GIs from seeking medical care. Service members returning from Iraq or Afghanistan with injuries or illnesses frequently find that getting to a doctor is difficult and obtaining treatment once there is no easier. Although military medicine has always had problems, the system has never been in such crisis. This situation is not something inherent in the military or in warfare but rather the result of the services' failure to maintain troop strength to sustain two long wars.

This chapter examines several of the problems soldiers face in obtaining medical care and in receiving proper benefits when they are medically unfit to serve. Although we focus on the psychiatric problems associated with these wars—post-traumatic stress disorder, or PTSD, in particular—the problems are no different for soldiers with physical injuries or other medical problems for which the military has promised care. The chapter begins with the frightening story of the Army's mistreatment of an officer who developed psychiatric difficulties in Iraq, and then describes a number of similar problems throughout the system. The parallels to the Vietnam era, particularly in the military's mishandling of PTSD and other psychiatric problems, are fairly well known, so we have not given this history a separate section. The chapter ends with a discussion of the current regulations governing medical care and medical discharges, and the ways in which soldiers, veterans, and progressive vets organizations are fighting back against mistreatment.

Tens of thousands of Vietnam veterans returned from war with serious physical problems and deep psychological scars. Many of them were unable to find work. They soon accounted for the majority of homeless veterans. Their psychological problems were often dismissed as "battle fatigue" or "shell shock" and frequently left untreated. Early reports showed psychiatric casualties at low levels, but these results turned out to be misleading. In 1980 PTSD finally joined the lexicon as a recognized category of illness with the publication of the third edition of the American Psychiatric Association's *Diagnostic and Statistical Manual of Mental Disorders* (DSM-III). Fifty-eight thousand U.S. troops were killed in Vietnam, but experts think more than that have committed suicide since the war ended, mainly as a result of PTSD.

The lessons of Vietnam were largely ignored by the Bush administration. The military has not maintained an adequate medical care system to minimize fatalities and provide prompt and thorough treatment for serious injuries and severe psychological disorders. Military officials "didn't anticipate the amount of patient care" the war would bring, said Col. Ronald Hamilton, commander of the medical center brigade at Walter Reed Army Medical Center.[1]

The real crime is that the military *knew* it could be facing this medical situation. The sort of normal military planning that happens in the Department of Defense takes into account high casualty rates and budgets for increased medical needs. Health care system weaknesses observed in prior wars are used in future planning. The military's frequent response to critics of the war in Iraq—that it could not have anticipated the extent and duration of the war—is simply disingenuous. This crisis was not accidental or the result of inability to anticipate the magnitude of the war, as DoD has long planned for wars of that sort. The Pentagon was well aware that it must have plans in place for heavy casualties and that PTSD would be a critical issue, but it chose not to make medical response a priority, focusing instead on weapons development and other concerns. Militaries are supposed to be prepared for wars.

Unprepared, DoD has failed to provide care for combat troops and other GIs with a range of injuries and illnesses. Many leave the military without diagnosis and treatment and return to civilian society lacking proper medical care or benefits to rebuild their lives. As a result tens of thousands of soldiers and veterans face difficult futures, and our society will pay the social and economic costs of these wars for generations to come.

The Story of Elizabeth Whiteside

Elizabeth Whiteside joined the Army Reserve after high school and participated in the Reserve Officer Training Corps (ROTC) while studying economics at the University of Virginia. After graduation in 2006, she was commissioned as an officer and assigned to Walter Reed Army Medical Center. That fall, she was deployed to Iraq and began working at the Camp Cropper detainee prison in Baghdad.

First Lieutenant Whiteside and some other female soldiers were involved in conflicts with a male officer who, they thought, had blocked female promotions and undercut Whiteside's authority with her soldiers. As tensions grew, Whiteside developed panic attacks and couldn't sleep, so she began self-medicating with NyQuil and Benadryl. Whiteside didn't seek help at the mental health clinic because she was afraid the Army would send her home.

After she took charge of quelling prison riots at Camp Cropper following the execution of Saddam Hussein, Whiteside had another confrontation with the problem officer, and she subsequently suffered a mental breakdown. She grew more agitated and at one point pushed away a nurse who tried to take the gun she was carrying. Lieutenant Whiteside fired twice at the ceiling, shouted that she wanted to kill the nurses, and eventually shot herself in the stomach.

Returned to Walter Reed, Whiteside was placed in a psychiatric unit and diagnosed with a severe major depressive disorder, a personality disorder, and dissociation from reality. But instead of treating its officer with compassion and empathy, the Army charged Whiteside with criminal offenses, including assault on a superior commissioned officer, aggravated assault, kidnapping, reckless endangerment, wrongful discharge of a firearm, communication of a threat, and attempted intentional self-injury without intent to avoid service.

While waiting for the Army to determine whether to court-martial her, Whiteside tried to kill herself. She swallowed dozens of antidepressants and other pills, leaving a note that said, "I'm very disappointed with the Army. Hopefully this will help other soldiers." Fortunately, Whiteside survived, and the Army dropped the charges against her, probably in response to media inquiries and public outrage about her treatment.[2]

The PTSD and Suicide Epidemics

One of the most tragic blunders of the wars in Iraq and Afghanistan is the military's failure to plan for the proliferation of post-traumatic stress disorder. According to the *Diagnostic and Statisti-*

cal Manual, PTSD is likely to occur as the result of "a traumatic event in which . . . the person experienced, witnessed, or was confronted with an event or events that involved actual or threatened death or serious injury, or a threat to the physical integrity of self or others, [and] the person's response involved intense fear, helplessness, or horror." Symptoms of PTSD can include reexperiencing the trauma through memories or flashbacks and retreating from life or a feeling of detachment, along with hypervigilance, impaired concentration, depression, and anxiety.

After he returned from Iraq, Specialist Jeans Cruz saw recurring images of dead Iraqi children. He heard voices and smelled stale blood. Cruz slashed his forearms to relive the pain and adrenaline of combat. Jeans Cruz has been diagnosed with "severe and chronic" PTSD.

Another Iraq Army veteran, 1st Lt. Jullian Philip Goodrum, imagines snipers with their sights trained on him in the street; diesel fumes cause him to have flashbacks. Former sergeant Matt LaBranche's memories of the nine months he spent in Iraq as a machine gunner in the Army left him "feeling dead inside." LaBranche struggles with images of an Iraqi woman dying in his arms after he shot her and of children who caught some of the bullets. "I'm taking enough drugs to sedate an elephant," LaBranche said, "and I still wake up dreaming about it. I wish I had just freaking died over there."[3]

"They ranged from little babies to adult males and females. I'll never be able to get that out of my head. I can still smell the blood. This left something in my head and heart," Lance Corporal Roel Ryan Briones said after the Haditha massacre. On November 19, 2005, Marines from Kilo Company, 3rd Battalion, 1st Marine Regiment, 1st Marine Division, based at Camp Pendleton killed 24 unarmed civilians in Haditha, Iraq, in a three- to five-hour rampage. The victims included a 76-year-old amputee in a wheelchair holding a Koran and a mother and child bent over as if in prayer.

Briones did not participate in the massacre, but he was ordered to take photographs of the victims and remove their bodies from their homes. He is still haunted by his memories of that day. Briones described picking up a young girl who was shot in the head. "I held her out like this," he said, extending his arms, "but her head was bobbing up and down and the insides fell on my legs. I used to be one of those Marines who said that post-traumatic stress is a bunch of bull," said Briones, who began having serious psychological problems when he returned home. "But all this stuff that keeps going through my head is eating me up."[4]

A July 2004 report in the *New England Journal of Medicine* found "a strong reported relation between combat experiences, such as being shot at, handling dead bodies, knowing someone who was killed, or killing enemy combatants, and the prevalence of PTSD." The risk of developing PTSD rises in direct proportion to the number of fire fights a soldier experiences.[5]

Unlike service members in prior wars, all troops in Iraq and Afghanistan, not just combat infantry, are exposed to civilian deaths and roadside bombs. "We call it '360-365' combat," explained Paul Sullivan, executive director of Veterans for Common Sense. That means that "veterans are completely surrounded by combat for one year," he said. "Nearly all of our soldiers are under fire, or being subjected to mortar rounds or roadside bombs, or witnessing the deaths of civilians or fellow soldiers."[6] Col. Charles W. Hoge of the division of psychiatry and neuroscience at Walter Reed concurs. "There is no front line in Iraq. Individuals who are patrolling the streets will be at higher risk of being involved in combat, but folks who are largely located at one base are also targets of mortar and artillery, and everyone in convoys is a target."[7]

PTSD is a leading diagnosis for mental health disorders of veterans returning from Iraq. During 2003–2005, there was a 232 percent increase in PTSD diagnoses for veterans who were born after 1972. An important study by the RAND Corporation estimated that 300,000 soldiers who had deployed to Iraq and Afghanistan "currently suffer from PTSD or major depression." Women and reservists have the highest incidence of PTSD and major depression.[8] Experts acknowledge that figures like this are low: the reality is significantly worse, masked by command and peer pressures not to report illness and misdiagnosis by military and VA physicians.

The high rate of PTSD among Iraq veterans results from a number of factors, including multiple deployments, the inability to identify the enemy, the lack of real safe zones, and the inadvertent killing of civilians. Some mental health experts feel that PTSD is intensified when soldiers do not feel their actions were justified, that is, when they do not believe they fought in a good cause.

Soldiers can suffer mild traumatic brain injury from a blow to the head or by being in close proximity to an explosion. A strong correlation has been shown between brain injuries and PTSD. The RAND study found that 320,000 individuals "experienced a probable TBI [traumatic brain injury] during deployment." Approximately one in six combat troops returning from Iraq have suffered at least one mild traumatic brain injury, according to a January 2008 report. These injuries can heighten the risk of physical and mental symptoms including sleeplessness, headaches, balance problems, and PTSD. Almost 44 percent of soldiers who blacked out had PTSD, a rate approximately three times that found in soldiers with other injuries. "Traumatic brain injury has been labeled a signature injury of the wars in Iraq and Afghanistan," that report concluded.[9]

The VA is treating more head injuries than chest and abdominal wounds for the first time. A July 2005 estimate from Walter Reed found that two-thirds of soldiers wounded in Iraq who cannot immediately return to duty have suffered traumatic brain injuries.[10]

In November 2007 CBS News aired a stunning report based on a five-month investigation. It found that more veterans committed suicide in one year than had been killed in combat in Iraq.[11] Dr. Ira Katz, deputy chief of patient care services office for mental health for the VA, wrote in an internal VA e-mail dated December 15, 2007, "There are about 18 suicides per day among America's 25 million veterans."[12] That rate adds up to an astounding 126 suicides per week, or 6,552 a year.

Tim Bowman was an Army reservist who patrolled Airport Road, one of the most dangerous places in Baghdad. "His eyes when he came back were just dead," said Bowman's mother. "The light wasn't there anymore." Eight months later, at the age of 23, Bowman shot himself. Derek Henderson jumped off a bridge after serving three tours of duty in Iraq.[13]

Chris Dana returned from Iraq in 2005 and began to isolate himself, missing family events, football games, and weekend duty. The Montana National Guard initiated a discharge for Dana under other-than-honorable conditions. Neither his family nor the guard noticed Dana sinking into a mental abyss. In March 2006 the 23-year-old shot himself in the head with a .22-caliber rifle.[14]

Dr. Stephen Rathbun, the interim head of the Department of Epidemiology and Biostatistics at the University of Georgia, concluded that in 2005 the suicide rate among male veterans 20 to 24 years old was three or four times the nonveteran rate in that age group.[15] According to a February 2008 report of the Department of Veterans Affairs' Office of Environmental Epidemiology, more than half the veterans who killed themselves after returning from Iraq or Afghanistan were members of the reserves or National Guard.[16] (That study didn't include soldiers who took their own lives in war zones or who stayed in the military after they returned home from the war.)

The epidemic of suicides and attempted suicides will be one of the most shameful legacies of the Bush administration's wars. Another is the deficiency in treatment our wounded service members receive.

The Failure of Military Medical Care

In theory service members are entitled to full medical care, and commands as well as doctors have an obligation to ensure that medical problems are addressed. Yet the rush to train and deploy troops to Iraq and Afghanistan has led many commands to ignore medical problems. Soldiers who complain about pain or request a visit to sick call are frequently harassed, labeled weaklings or whiners, and even accused of malingering. Many service members are reluctant to seek medical services because they fear being stigmatized or facing negative career repercussions. The RAND study cited earlier recommends that policies be changed so there are no perceived or real adverse career consequences for individuals who seek treatment, except when functional impairment compromises fitness for duty.

Pfc. Jason Scheuerman was a troubled soldier in Iraq who placed the muzzle of his weapon in his mouth on several occasions. After he was found sitting with his weapon between his legs and bobbing his head on the muzzle, Scheuerman's rifle and ammunition were taken from him. He indicated on a mental health questionnaire that he was anxious, uptight, and depressed; had feelings of hopelessness and despair; and thought about taking his life. He told the psychologist he did not have suicidal thoughts but also said things that suggested he was hallucinating. The psychologist told Scheuerman's commanders to return him to his unit because he may have been feigning mental illness to get out the Army. Scheuerman nailed a suicide note to his barracks closet, then stepped inside and shot and killed himself.[17]

Supervisors often press soldiers to keep quiet about injuries, to "suck it up" and continue their duties. Although they have no authority to prohibit medical care, these same supervisors frequently forbid GIs to go to sick call or keep scheduled medical appointments. Needless to say, forgoing treatment can exacerbate many injuries, sometimes causing permanent damage.

Soldiers who make their way to sick call must get through a "gatekeeper" system that could give HMOs lessons in denial of care. Although many corpsmen and medics are highly competent and caring professionals, they are frequently swamped with cases and under pressure to return soldiers to training or duty as soon as possible. And though always a problem, underdiagnosis of less-than-obvious injuries and illnesses reaches serious proportions in wartime. Diagnoses like lower-back pain, pain syndrome, and sprains are often made without thorough examination or radiological imaging that would reveal more serious problems.

GIs with symptoms of serious emotional distress are often underdiagnosed with adjustment disorders, which are relatively mild psychiatric conditions that are expected to resolve in a short time with limited treatment. PTSD among returning combat troops is frequently misdiagnosed as personality disorder; investigations at Fort Carson found a disturbing pattern of erroneous personality disorder diagnoses among returning troops, often after a single 15-minute interview. Many of these cases were later diagnosed by the VA as PTSD. Misdiagnosis of more serious conditions as personality disorders is a problem of long standing, but it has become more common during the current wars. It may be noteworthy that, unlike a great many psychological problems, personality disorders do not warrant medical compensation from the military or the VA. Unfortunately, personality disorder is also the only psychological disorder that is named on the DD-214 discharge document; such a designation creates a stigma for many veterans.

Public and congressional concern about this problem has become so great that in August 2008 the DoD revised its discharge regulation to require a second opinion and review by the surgeon general's office whenever a personality disorder diagnosis is given to a soldier who is serving or has served in an "imminent danger" pay zone.[18]

Former Army sergeant Kristofer Goldsmith didn't receive his PTSD diagnosis from the VA until months after he attempted suicide, the day before he was scheduled to deploy to Iraq for a second tour. "While undergoing psychiatric treatment, I heard of many people being diagnosed with personality disorder and adjustment disorder instead of PTSD," he said. "I believe this is a way for the Army to hide the levels of PTSD among its ranks."[19]

Such failures to diagnose serious illness led Congress to demand extensive screening of soldiers before and after deployment to Iraq. Pre- and postdeployment screening is now mandatory, but GIs report that the screening, when done, is often haphazard enough to miss significant problems.

The military's medical system is stretched beyond its endurance. Particularly in the Army, lack of medical personnel and proper facilities has left many soldiers languishing in poor conditions while waiting for care or disability retirement proceedings. The scandal at Walter Reed Army Medical Center, once considered the crown jewel of Army hospitals, illustrates the situation. In early 2007 at the urging of veterans groups, investigative journalists reported that about 700 seriously ill or injured soldiers and Marines went months without adequate care in unsanitary and dilapidated facilities at Walter Reed. These soldiers had been released from the hospital itself but were still in need of treatment or awaiting decisions on discharge or return to duty. Nursing care was minimal, and in many cases family members had to attend to routine care like bathing patients and changing their beds. Many became lost in the system; misplaced and inaccurate paperwork often caused the delays. Reporters at the *Washington Post* estimated that soldiers faced an average delay of ten months.[20]

Acute hospital care at Walter Reed is far better but not without problems. For example, the "lack of early identification techniques" at Walter Reed as well as at the National Naval Medical Center in Bethesda, MD, led to "inconsistent diagnosis and treatment" of veterans with PTSD and traumatic brain injury, according to an April 2007 Department of Defense report.[21]

Long waits at Walter Reed reflected extreme problems in the Army's disability evaluation system (DES), which determines whether service members are medically fit and processes for disability discharge or retirement those who are unfit. Large and increasing numbers of cases have clogged the system, and Army authorities admit it is in crisis; some critics more accurately label it "broken." The Navy DES, which processes Marine as well as Navy cases, has not been as heavily burdened but is still affected by the wars.

Lengthy delays are not the only problem. Misdiagnosis and underdiagnosis frequently result in underrating the degree of disability, which determines the amount of compensation soldiers receive if they are medically discharged or retired. In addition, Army disability awards are often lower than those given in the other services for identical medical conditions. These problems were investigated in 2007 and 2008, and some improvements have been made, but the system is still seriously troubled, and individual soldiers are often denied essential medical benefits.

The Redeployment of Unfit Troops

One of the worst aspects of the current situation is the widespread redeployment of soldiers with serious physical injuries, brain damage, and debilitating psychological wounds. The military is so desperate for troops that it is sending soldiers back to the front who are not fit to fight. Since 2003 over 43,000 U.S. troops who were listed as medically unfit for combat before their deployment to Afghanistan or Iraq were deployed anyway, according to the Pentagon.[22] In many cases mentally ill soldiers are prescribed psychotropic medications and given little or no monitoring, then returned to combat, often with disastrous consequences.

On January 3, 2008, Capt. Scot Tebo, the surgeon for Fort Carson's 3rd Brigade Combat Team, acknowledged in an e-mail obtained by the *Denver Post*, "We have been having issues reaching deployable strength, and thus have been taking along some borderline soldiers who we would otherwise have left behind for continued treatment." Indeed, Master Sgt. Denny Nelson, a 19-year Army veteran with a serious foot injury, was sent overseas in December 2007 despite doctors' orders that he not jump, run, or carry more than 20 pounds for three months. Major Thomas Schymanski, a physician in Kuwait, sent an e-mail to Tebo urging him to send Nelson home: "This soldier should NOT have even left CONUS (the United States) . . . In his current state, he is not full mission capable and in his current condition is a risk to further injury to himself, others and his unit." Nelson was returned to the United States.[23]

Another Fort Carson soldier being treated at a hospital for bipolar disorder and alcohol abuse after attempting suicide was released early and ordered to deploy to the Middle East in late 2007. After 31 days in Kuwait, he was sent back to Fort Carson when health care professionals in Kuwait agreed that he had bipolar disorder and "some paranoia and possible homicidal tendencies," according to additional e-mails the *Denver Post* acquired.[24]

In May 2006 the *Hartford Courant* released the results of an investigation that documented numerous instances in which troops with serious psychological problems were sent to Iraq. Some mentally ill soldiers were kept in a war zone on antidepressants and antianxiety drugs with little or no medical monitoring, in violation of military regulations. The *Courant's* study described cases in which soldiers were maintained in combat even after their superiors were warned about suicide risks and other signs of mental illness. This report opened the door to other studies about the redeployment of mentally ill soldiers and the misuse of psychotropic medication on troops.[25]

Pfc. David Potter was diagnosed with depression and anxiety while serving with the Army in Iraq in 2004, yet he remained on active duty in Baghdad. After a suicide attempt, a psychiatrist recommended that he be released from the Army. Ten days later, Potter shot and killed himself. Spec. Jeffrey Henthorn's superiors in the Army knew that he had twice threatened to commit suicide. Nevertheless, Henthorn was sent back to Iraq, where he shot and killed himself with his rifle in 2005.[26]

The *Courant* reported that the Army's leading mental health expert admitted that the redeployment of service members with PTSD has been driven partly by the shortage of troops. "The challenge for us is that the Army has a mission to fight," Col. Elspeth C. Ritchie said in 2006. "And as you know, recruiting has been a challenge." Stephen Robinson, former director of the National Gulf War Resource Center, echoed Ritchie's comments. "What you have is a military stretched so thin, they've resorted to keeping psychologically unfit soldiers at the front. It's a policy that can do an awful lot of damage over time."[27]

After service members returning from the first Gulf war reported illnesses the military said were unrelated to combat, Congress passed a law in 1997 that requires the military to conduct a mental health assessment on all troops before deployment. But this assessment consisted of a single mental health question on a form, and even soldiers who reported on that form that they had psychological problems rarely obtained referrals to mental health professionals. Troops who received a positive evaluation for possible mental illness were found to be fit for service 85 percent of the time; over 93 percent of those who screened positive were never referred for a mental health evaluation. Although the military admits that more than 9 percent of those deployed have serious psychological illnesses, fewer than 1 percent receive evaluations from mental health professionals.[28] Command pressure to deploy has circumvented most efforts to improve screening.

Further congressional action and additional DoD regulations have done little to solve the problem. The 2005 National Defense Authorization Act again required careful screening of deploying troops.[29] In January 2006 DoD issued a new directive, Individual Medical Readiness, designed to ensure effective screening and accurate decision making about deployment of troops with medical conditions.[30] Less than a year later, to meet the requirements of the 2007 Defense Authorization Act, DoD created a new policy memorandum with more detailed guidelines, which listed psychiatric conditions and medications that would prohibit deployment or require a three-month delay in deployment to ensure patients were stable enough to deploy.[31] Periodic announcements from DoD and Army officials tout improvements in screening, but many GIs still face deployment with diagnoses of serious psychiatric disorders.

Army psychiatrist Col. Hoge told Congress in March 2008 that the current period of 12 months between combat tours of duty "is insufficient time" for troops "to reset" from combat stress before they return to the war. Hoge said almost 30 percent of soldiers on their third deployment have serious mental health problems. "Are we trying to bandage up what is essentially an insufficient fighting force?" asked Dr. Frank Ochberg, a long-time psychiatrist and member of the board of the International Society for Traumatic Stress Studies.[32]

In the course of her counseling work, one of the authors, Kathleen Gilberd, continues to see people who have been diagnosed a few weeks or even days before deployment, put on medications like Paxil or Prozac, and deployed on schedule, despite DoD requirements. GIs are being deployed when there is no way to tell whether their potentially serious depression will abate or become more severe.

Time magazine reported in June 2008 that "for the first time in history, a sizable and growing number of U.S. combat troops are taking daily doses of antidepressants to calm nerves strained by repeated and lengthy tours in Iraq and Afghanistan." In March 2008 the Army's fifth Mental Health Advisory Team estimated that about 12 percent of combat troops in Iraq and 17 percent of troops in Afghanistan are taking prescription antidepressants such as Prozac and Zoloft or sleeping pills like Ambien to cope. The number is higher in Afghanistan because of escalating violence there and the greater isolation of the mission.[33]

Military Medicine published a paper in July 2007 by three military psychiatrists that encouraged military doctors deploying to Iraq and Afghanistan to "request a considerable quantity of the SSRI [a class of antidepressants] they are most comfortable prescribing" for "treatment of new-onset depressive disorders" in the war zones in order "to 'conserve the fighting strength'" (the motto of the Army Medical Corps).[34]

But "you can't start someone on antidepressants and then not see them again because their unit is moving around," said Sandy Moreno, who served in Iraq as a psychiatric technician in the Army Reserve. "When you put them on those kinds of meds, a lot of times it takes six weeks before they take effect, or they can cause side effects. We could never keep that good track of a soldier."[35]

Once soldiers receive a profile indicating they have a permanent or chronic medical condition that may require significant limitations in assignment, Army guidance generally requires further evaluation of the soldiers' ability to perform duties in their current job assignments. DoD policy states that all soldiers are to be evaluated for medical readiness prior to deployment. Yet the U.S. Government Accountability Office concluded in its June 2008 report, "Army requirements for deploying soldiers with medical conditions are not always being met; commanders are not always aware of medical limitations in a timely way, and . . . commanders are not always adhering to guidance to ensure that soldiers are not being deployed to Iraq or Afghanistan" prior to undergoing proper evaluations.[36]

The Regulations: GIs and Veterans Fight Back

Fortunately, GIs have some rights in the military's medical and disability evaluation systems, although, as with other rights, local commands often claim they don't exist. In fact, soldiers can use the same regulations and grievance procedures that protect the right to dissent in order to protest inadequate medical care and benefits. Individual soldiers have the right to complain through the commands and through the medical system, and to bring these issues to the attention of members of Congress and the media. They can demand improvements in the system and proper handling of their own cases.

Traditional complaint procedures, such as those set out in Article 138 of the Uniform Code of Military Justice or that of going to the inspector general (IG), and other complaint methods discussed in Chapter 4, may be effective when commands deny access to medical care. The military's medical regulations can be used to demand proper care and evaluation of disabilities. Medical regulations, including DoD Instruction 1332.38, and implementing service regulations, establish protocols for medical treatment and list medical conditions that warrant referral to the disability evaluation system for limited duty, discharge, or medical retirement.[37] Although the military's medical ombudsman system has not proved of great use, physicians and others in the military's medical corps are subject to the UCMJ and their own regulations, so administrative complaints through the medical chain of command and IG complaints are sometimes effective.

In addition, GIs have extensive rights in the disability evaluation system. Standards for medical discharge and retirement are governed by statute.[38] Department of Defense Instruction 1332.18 and implementing service regulations allow service members to rebut and appeal the findings of medical boards and the fitness and disability rating decisions of the Physical Evaluation Boards (PEBs).[39] The military provides information through a system of Physical Evaluation Board liaison officers and, for those whose cases go to formal PEB hearings, military attorneys. But this help is often too little, too late.

Assistance from civilian attorneys and military counseling groups is always useful. Frequently, military doctors do not tell GIs whether or not their cases are being considered for medical retirement or discharge until the doctors have made the initial decision to prepare a Medical Evaluation Board (MEB) report. And they are given little information about these essential proceedings—medical conclusions in MEBs and determinations about discharge, retirement, and compensation by the PEBs—until they are well underway. GIs often waive important rights or fail to challenge inaccurate diagnoses and disability ratings because they were not given enough information to know they had any reason to do so. Advocates suggest that service members seek outside help when they first discover they have medical problems, rather than waiting until they encounter legal problems in their treatment or disability proceedings.

GIs with medical problems can find information about rights and procedures in the military's own regulations. In addition, a wealth of information is available on supportive Web sites, including the GI Rights Network's GIRightsHotline.org and the Military Law Task Force's NLGMLTF.org. Civilian attorneys and counselors often represent service members in these proceedings, coming in well before military attorneys would be available and assisting long after military legal help ends. GIs who are unaware of their rights or unsuccessful in asserting them in the military can request benefits later from the VA, which is not bound by military diagnoses or disability decisions, and can appeal the military's determinations through the Boards for Correction of Military Records.

During and after the war in Vietnam, veterans groups and military counseling organizations played a key role in the fight for veterans' and GIs' rights to proper medical care and benefits. Progressive veterans organizations struggled for recognition of, and VA compensation for, Vietnam's mystery diseases—which were later traced to exposure to Agent Orange herbicide sprayed in Vietnam—and for PTSD. Organizations like Vietnam Veterans Against the War, Vietnam Veterans of America, and legal companion groups like the National Veterans Legal Services Program (NVLSP) and the Veterans Education Project (VEP) pressed for reforms in the VA and the military and for help for veterans who received bad discharges as the result of medical and psychological problems. GIs who had been active in antiwar and antiracist organizing took up veterans' rights issues and brought important political analysis and insights to that work, educating the public about the relationship between mistreatment of GIs and veterans and the war in Vietnam.

These groups helped set up legal clinics and trained advocates to represent veterans in VA proceedings for benefit claims and in upgrading bad discharges; other than honorable discharges meant loss of veterans' benefits, and upgrading them could be critical for those whose problems had not been recognized in the military. The groups pressed the military to improve its conservative Discharge Review Boards and Board for Correction of Military Records. NVLSP, the VEP, the American GI Forum, Swords to Plowshares (STP), and other groups trained advocates in these systems and represented thousands of veterans with medical and other problems still common today. These problems include underdiagnosis and misdiagnosis of medical and psychological problems, punitive treatment of drug addiction and self-medication with alcohol, and stigmatization of discharges limiting job opportunities and VA benefits. Legal manuals and self-help materials created during that period allowed veterans to become their own advocates as well.

THE MEDICAL SIDE OF WAR · 147

Today the growing GI movement and progressive veterans groups have begun to play the same role. Vietnam Veterans Against the War provides assistance with VA claims and discharge upgrades to new veterans. Iraq Veterans Against the War made medical care for soldiers and veterans one of its principal goals; along with immediate withdrawal of U.S. troops from Iraq and reparations for the Iraqi people, IVAW demands "full benefits, adequate health care (including mental care), and other support for returning servicemen and women." The failures of military medical care are reported in GIs' underground electronic newsletters; Courage to Resist includes in its roster of resisters a number of GIs who have gone AWOL or moved to Canada because of medical mistreatment. The civilian counseling movement and groups like the Military Law Task Force have taken up this issue earlier in today's wars than legal groups did during the Vietnam War, in part because of the lessons learned from that era's GI and veterans movements.

NVLSP (at www.nvlsp.org), STP (at www.swords-to-plowshares .org), the Military Law Task Force, and some of the other " oldtimers" are still around, providing important resources and training, while more recent veterans groups have joined the effort. Veterans for America (at www.veteransforamerica.org), which includes Vietnam veterans in its leadership, helped to expose the crises at Walter Reed and other military hospitals, and has published a lengthy and detailed online self-help book, *American Veterans and Servicemembers Survival Guide.* These and other organizations assist veterans in navigating the VA system and seeking upgrades of bad discharges or requesting medical retirement where the military has ignored serious medical problems and discharged GIs for personality disorders or misconduct.

Veterans groups have encouraged serious investigative reporting and repeated congressional inquiries about the military's efforts to hide the medical problems caused by the wars, the failure of military medical care, the Army's broken disability system, and the weaknesses of the VA. More GIs, veterans, and family members are joining this effort, which represents a groundswell of anger at the system and determination to press for the rights and benefits promised and denied by the military. Although these efforts cannot undo the terrible damage caused by the wars, they can limit the government's ability to cover up the problems and its refusal to respond to the needs of soldiers and veterans. Thanks to groups like IVAW and Courage to Resist, many soldiers and civilians are beginning to consider the connection between the military's failure to provide health care and benefits and the wars that underlie that failure, and to include both issues in protests and disengagement.

· EIGHT ·

Discharges

MANY SERVICE MEMBERS disengage from the military by seeking early discharge. A number of honorable discharges are available under military regulations, though soldiers rarely learn this from the military itself.

Discharge is a dirty word in most commands. Soldiers hear, over and over, that they can't quit, no matter what the circumstances or problem, no matter how they feel about the job or the wars they are being asked to fight. Many GIs request discharge when they learn that the duties and benefits recruiters promised them were lies. Others decide to get out when personal or family problems make it necessary for them to go home or when medical difficulties render it impossible to perform their duties. Like the service members discussed in earlier chapters, many ask to leave when they conclude that the mission is illegal, immoral, or dishonorable.

The first thing most GIs hear is "no." Regardless of circumstances, regulations, or qualification for discharge, drill instructors, supervisors, and commanders routinely say discharge is impossible. Their answer to any problem is often, "You signed a contract. You live with it." This response is almost automatic, but it is also wrong.

This response is especially common in wartime, when personnel needs are high and replacements are hard to find. Soldiers often hear that all discharges, or at least the discharge they seek, will be deferred until the end of the war. GIs hear that stop-loss policies prevent early discharge, although such discharges are exempted from the stop-loss regs. Asking for discharge is often treated as cowardly or disloyal. GIs who want out are told that they aren't really men (or, in the case of women, that they're worthless) and that they are turning their backs on fellow soldiers and their country.

Early discharges are quite legal. They are part and parcel of military regulations, and service members are routinely discharged before the end of active obligated service (EAOS) for a wide variety of reasons. But most GIs who receive early discharges were first told that it was impossible, and many had to go to civilian sources to learn the criteria and procedures for discharge. GIs receive little or no information about this topic during training, except for warnings about other than honorable discharges for things like AWOL, illegal drug use, and other misconduct. Because of this lack of information, some GIs choose to go AWOL, commit misconduct, or even injure themselves to get out, because the military has left them unaware of other discharges that may fit them perfectly and avoid legal problems or harm.

Conscientious objection discharge was discussed in Chapter 2, and medical discharge and retirement in Chapter 7. This chapter considers one soldier's successful effort to get a hardship discharge despite hindrance from his command. We scrutinize discharges generally and explain the procedures for several discharges by way of examples. We pay special attention to a pre–active duty discharge, separation from the Delayed Entry Program (DEP) or Delayed Training Program (DTP), which recruits can obtain before they take a second enlistment oath and report for active duty. By way of a little history, we examine the GI counseling movement, which grew into maturity during the Vietnam era, kept going afterward, and has now blossomed again since the invasion of Iraq.

A Soldier's Hardship

José Crespa joined the Army in 2006. He was assigned to a unit at Fort Carson in Colorado and then deployed to Iraq. Home on leave over the 2007 Christmas holidays, Crespa discovered that his family was in crisis. His adult sister had developed serious psychiatric problems. His mother, in poor health with diabetes and other problems, was the only one available to care for her. Crespa's mother was forced to quit work as her own medical condition became worse under the stress of caring for her daughter.

Knowing that his command would not be sympathetic to his situation, Crespa stayed home, AWOL, for four weeks to try to bring the problems under control. Then he turned himself in at Fort Carson, explained his family problems, and said that he needed a hardship discharge. The answer was an immediate no from his sergeant up to the major. A discharge was out of the question, they said, and besides, it could only be considered if he first went back to Iraq and applied from there. They also claimed that he couldn't be discharged because he had gone AWOL. If he didn't board a plane for Iraq, he would face court-martial and time in Leavenworth. At least once a day, a sergeant, staff sergeant, or officer came to tell him one or another of these claims, although he read the regulations and found that much of what they said was untrue.

Crespa politely stated that court-martial didn't matter because he had to take care of his family. He provided a letter from his mother's doctor, medical records, urgent messages from the Red

Cross, and when his sister was hospitalized, records from the hospital. His command just kept saying no. Crespa sought help from James Branum, an attorney with the Military Law Task Force, along with Kathleen Gilberd and a counselor, Dawn Blanken, from the GI Rights Network in Colorado. They helped him put together a discharge application, with more medical documentation, statements from family and friends, and his own formal statement. When the command left the application sitting on the wrong desk—claiming it could only be considered by his commander in Iraq but failing to forward it to the commander—the attorney helped him prepare a complaint under Article 138 of the Uniform Code of Military Justice (discussed in Chapter 4).

At one point, Crespa was ordered to board a plane to Iraq the next day, although an Army doctor had just labeled him a "no-go" because of the emotional distress the situation had caused. Crespa stayed put, patiently explaining that he wasn't cleared to leave and that he needed to go home to his family. He was finally granted some emergency leave after his sister was rushed to the hospital, where she was diagnosed with schizophrenia. But the leave was just for a few days, and though his sister was able to come home while he was there, she was soon back in the hospital.

The command continued to threaten Leavenworth, even posting a note on the unit bulletin board showing that he was scheduled for a general court-martial, the highest form of military court. Crespa continued to politely request discharge. When his attorney called the base legal office, he found that no such court-martial was under consideration. The legal office also became concerned when its staff learned that the hardship application, and now the complaint, had been misplaced. An Army lawyer had words with the command.

Although the command tried a few more threats, his supervisor realized that Crespa was not going to give up. At the suggestion of Crespa's attorney, a reporter from the *Denver Post* called the command to inquire about Crespa's situation. The command discovered that his attorney and counselors were serious about pursuing the Article 138 complaint, along with a new complaint for failure to answer the first complaint by the deadline in the regulations. Suddenly the threats of court-martial ended. Crespa was given light punishment for his AWOL at a nonjudicial punishment hearing. The charge of refusing orders to deploy had disappeared. Almost five months after his return to the base, Crespa walked out the gate with a fully honorable discharge by reason of hardship.

Reasons for Discharges

Military regulations include a number of discharges, many of which would be news to most service members. In addition to regulations on conscientious objection discharge and medical discharge, the Department of Defense requires commands to follow a DoD instruction and service regulations in granting a number of other discharges.[1] GIs can request discharges in cases of:

- family hardship or dependency
- parenthood, for single parents or families with both parents in the service who cannot adequately care for a child
- pregnancy or childbirth
- entry-level performance and conduct problems (problems adapting) during the first 180 days of training
- "don't ask, don't tell," formally called "homosexual conduct"
- personality disorders, a group of specific psychological problems
- other physical or mental conditions not quite serious enough to require medical discharge

- erroneous enlistment (including contract violations, recruiter fraud, and even fraudulent enlistment)
- status as an alien
- surviving family member (formerly called sole surviving son)
- unsatisfactory performance of duties
- separation from the Delayed Entry Program (DEP) or Delayed Training Program (DTP)

Several other administrative discharges are available as well. All of these are honorable or general under honorable conditions (also called general), or uncharacterized entry-level separations for recruits in their first 180 days of training. Some of these discharges may be requested directly. Others are described as involuntary and are supposed to be initiated by commands, though service members can provide the evidence that discharge is warranted and, if necessary, can request the discharge themselves or through outside advocates.

In addition, the command can initiate discharges that are usually under other than honorable (OTH) conditions, including misconduct, illegal drug use, discharge in lieu of court-martial, and several other reasons specified in the regulations; these discharges are normally best avoided.

Although the military doesn't talk about these regulations, a number of independent military counseling groups and attorneys experienced in military law provide information about discharges, links to the discharge regulations, and assistance in handling the discharge process. The GI Rights Network (at www.girights hotline.org, toll-free hotline 877-447-4487), offers information and counseling to demystify the discharge criteria and procedures and provide practical information about documentation to support discharges. The Military Law Task Force (at www.nlgmltf.org) offers information and resources. These groups and other counseling organizations are discussed later in this chapter and listed in Resources in the Appendix. They offer much more information than one chapter can cover, but a few examples of common discharges may help clarify the difference between the myth that "you can't quit" and the reality of discharges.

As noted, GIs with serious family problems may request discharge for hardship or dependency.[2] The criteria are fairly straightforward. A member of the GI's immediate family must have a severe medical, psychological, or financial hardship that cannot be controlled or solved without the service member's presence. The GI, and no one else, must be able to solve the problem or keep it from becoming much worse. The hardship must have arisen or become worse since the GI's enlistment, and, finally, it must be one of long duration. Long duration usually means that the hardship will not resolve for at least a year; short-term problems are handled with hardship transfers (compassionate reassignments) instead of discharge.

Documentation and processing of this discharge take work: GIs and their families must gather extensive evidence from doctors (in medical cases), prospective employers (in financial hardships), family members, neighbors, friends, or others to prove that the hardship is real and meets all of the criteria. The evidence must show that the soldier is needed (in medical cases some services require that a doctor recommended this). A written job offer and detailed budget are necessary if the hardship is financial. The person with the hardship and other family members must write consistent and fairly detailed accounts that describe the problem, the soldier's ability to solve it, and the absence of any alternatives. Sometimes services want verification of the hardship through the Red Cross.

Fortunately, the discharge regulations provide a description of the documentation, and counselors or attorneys can help interpret the regs, suggest types of documentation, and review prepared documentation for clarity and consistency. Some counselors suggest that, contrary to the regs, commands tend to weigh hardships according to the amount of documentation provided. Although most hardship discharge applicants do not tell their commands they have help, outside legal assistance often proves invaluable in these cases.

Once submitted, paperwork may become lost or be returned because of simple typographical errors or a demand for more evidence, and senior enlisted personnel will sometimes claim they can deny the application on their own, although this is not true. Some commands set up hardship boards to assess the problems before the commander makes a recommendation and sends the matter to a commanding officer higher in the chain of command (the separation authority) for approval or denial. Attorneys and counselors familiar with this discharge say that claims are occasionally denied on ridiculous grounds or no grounds at all. But with persistence, thorough documentation, and outside legal help, GIs can be released for family hardship, and many are every year. If turned down, GIs can reapply with additional documentation, usually with evidence that the problem is becoming worse. Federal courts will sometimes order the discharge when commands have acted arbitrarily.

A second example is discharge under "don't ask, don't tell," the common name for the military's policy on "homosexual conduct."[3] The current version of the policy was initiated by the Clinton administration, then revised by Congress and reformulated in regulations. At heart it is similar to the military policy it replaced, and the ones before that. GIs who are gay, lesbian, or bisexual are supposed to be discharged if they reveal their sexual orientation to their commanders or others. Many seek discharge due to the difficulty of living and working silently in a homophobic environment or because of the war and other problems affecting all GIs.

Under the regs, being gay is not in itself a reason for discharge. But GIs' mere statements that they are gay or lesbian are grounds for discharge, as are broadly defined homosexual acts (almost any touching) and marriages. Discharges are honorable, general, or entry level, based on GIs' records of service, unless specific aggravating circumstances are present. These circumstances involve any acts that are committed, attempted, or solicited by use of force, coercion, or intimidation; with a person under age 16; with a subordinate in some circumstances; in public view, broadly defined; for money; aboard a military vessel or plane; or, under most circumstances, in any military location.

With this discharge outside legal assistance is extremely important because commands occasionally respond with improper investigations, threats of court-martial, or other reactions outside the regulations, and because harassment of known or suspected lesbians and gay men is still a problem in some places. Legal assistance is also important when GIs face discharge against their wishes. Each year hundreds of GIs are recommended for involuntary discharge for homosexual conduct, often on the basis of second-hand information, allegations, or rumors (an improper basis for discharge) their commands gained from other sources.

Military counselors and attorneys recommend that GIs who want this discharge give a written statement to their commands simply stating their sexual orientation. They always recommend that this statement be in writing to avoid misinterpretation or reinterpretation of what is said, and they recommend that the statement not include any information about sexual activity. Some discharge applicants explain how they feel about the policy or why military homophobia troubles them, and some explain that they are proud to be "out" or want to work for lesbian and gay rights. But this statement should always be reviewed by a counselor or attorney before it is submitted, and it may be accompanied by a letter from the counselor or attorney.

Counselors and attorneys also recommend that GIs provide their commands no further information. The regulations allow commands to conduct limited fact-finding inquiries when statements are made, though commands may skip this step if they know or believe the statement is true. If commands aren't convinced by the first written statement, a second written statement talking about nonsexual activities, but never about acts, can be submitted by the advocate. Current regulations do not allow investigations to go beyond the facts the command already has; when soldiers make statements about their orientation, commands can ask around about other statements but are not supposed to ask about their sex lives at all. Many commands have a hard time following this rule.

Some commands, particularly during wartime, don't want to believe gay discharge requests and assume or pretend they are false. Counselors have found that explanation of lesbian or gay activism or charitable work at a local gay rights center is usually enough "proof" for those commanders who can't believe a simple statement. Most also believe that no straight soldiers would step foot into local gay- and lesbian-identified places. If commands persist in ignoring the discharge, suggestions of litigation, inquiries from lesbian and gay rights organizations, or even hints of a press release (from the attorney or counselor, not the client!) about the command's willingness to retain openly gay service members are usually persuasive.

The command then formally notifies GIs that the policy requires discharge and informs them of their rights in the discharge proceedings. The command should forward the statement and these documents, with a command recommendation, up the chain of command for a decision. The services vary here: some send cases to military headquarters, and some use a base commander or the equivalent as the discharge authority. If the command acts properly, this discharge can be processed smoothly in a matter of weeks or a couple of months. Delays beyond that are usually the result of command inaction or mishandled paperwork.

During wartime gays and lesbians who wish to serve are often able to do so without threats of discharge. Harassment is also less common during wartime, but service members should beware of commands that make efforts to single out and harass, or involuntarily discharge, members they think are lesbian or gay. Under the watchful eye of the Servicemembers Legal Defense Network (SLDN, at www.sldn.org), and groups like the Military Law Task Force and the GI Rights Network, service members are more aware of their rights, and fewer witch hunt–style mass investigations and humiliating interrogations not based on facts have taken place. Groups like SLDN are often able to press commands to respond promptly and seriously to homophobic harassment and hate crimes. Nonetheless, homophobia is alive and well under the "don't ask, don't tell" policy.

Delayed Entry Program Discharges

Recruitment is of increasing concern to the military during these wars, as young men and women show less interest in enlistment. As a result, the military spends millions of dollars on slick advertising campaigns and sends recruiters into high schools and communities (video arcades are a favorite place) with promises of adventure and training in the service. Independent studies show that recruiters routinely lie about military benefits and programs to induce people to enlist. A number of families of minors have reported that they signed consents to enlistment only after being assured that the forms were consent forms for medical examinations or testing, not enlistment. High-pressure enlistment tactics are the norm.

To make enlistment more palatable, and to catch kids before they have even finished high school, the military offers delayed enlistments—DEP programs to enlist in the service months after signing a contract and a parallel DTP program for enlistment in the reserves. Recruits are told they can sign now and change their mind later.

In fact, many recruits do change their minds when they have a chance to think about enlistment or learn more about the reality of the recruiters' promises. Large numbers tell their recruiters that they have decided not to go, decided on college or a civilian job instead, or have realized medical problems or personal or family hardships make enlistment impossible. Some decide that they object to the current wars or that they are conscientious objectors, objecting to all wars.

Unsurprisingly, recruiters then tell recruits discharge is impossible or, in the alternative, that they must wait and report to basic training, after which they can easily apply for discharge. Kathleen Gilberd, who handles DEP discharges and other discharge cases, finds this to be one of the recruiters' most offensive lies, because discharges are difficult to obtain, though legally quite feasible, during basic training, when isolated and often frightened recruits are wrongly told they have waited too long to do anything about discharge.

But military regulations allow discharge from the DEP and DTP through a simple paperwork process prior to entry on active duty.[4] Under the regs recruits may be separated for family or personal problems much less significant than those triggering discharge for active duty personnel. Simple reasons like a change of career plans or enrollment in college are grounds for discharge, and the regulations contain provisions for those who simply do not want to go. Although recruiters will say that recruits have signed a binding contract, the enlistment agreements they sign are only enlistments in the inactive reserve; a second oath is taken before entering active duty. And the agreement binds recruits and the military alike to the regulations, which permit discharge.

These discharges are best handled by ignoring the immediate recruiter and requesting separation from the regional or district recruiting headquarters. Experience shows that these requests are given more serious attention when advocates or attorneys inform the recruit command that they represent the recruits in the discharge request.

Most counselors suggest that recruits write a simple statement requesting discharge and mentioning the problems or decisions that require them to seek separation. Some recruits, to be cautious, submit medical records, college acceptance letters, or other documents to support their claims. Advocates can submit an accompanying letter mentioning the regulations that govern discharges, explaining that the recruit does not wish to be contacted and referring all questions to an attorney. Under the regs the recruiting command is obliged to authorize separation if the recruit meets any of the many general reasons listed in the regulation.

The problem in these cases is not meeting the requirements for discharge, or even getting the district command to process the paperwork. Rather it is avoiding the recruiters who respond with threats and lies, warning that discharge is impossible and failure to enlist means a dishonorable discharge, court-martial, federal prison, or worse. None of these things are true, but young men and women, as well as their families, are often frightened by such threats. Counselors with the GI Rights Network have reported cases in which recruiters threatened to call police to have unwilling recruits arrested. In one reported case, a recruiter actually called the police, who responded, only to tell the recruiter hovering at the recruit's front door that they had no reason or authority to arrest the young man and that the recruiter should probably get off the property as the family requested. Other counselors have reported cases in which recruiters literally took recruits for a ride, telling them that they were driving to their office to sign discharge paperwork but in fact taking them to the local Military Entrance Processing Station (MEPS) for a physical; another, more important, oath; and delivery to boot camp.

Advocates suggest that the best approach is to avoid recruiters altogether, to deal only with their superiors at the district recruiting office, and to use a counselor or attorney as a buffer between the recruit and overzealous recruiters. Because discharge is entirely legal under the regs, only the recruiters' high-pressure tactics are available to overcome a determined "no."

Involuntary Discharges

Each year thousands of service members are forced out of the military through involuntary administrative discharges—almost always for personality disorder, misconduct, drug abuse, discharge in lieu of court-martial, or unsatisfactory participation in the reserves. Sometimes GIs are willing to accept the discharges, glad to get out despite the reason for and character of the discharge. In some cases GIs have given up and gone AWOL or committed other misconduct because they need to get out and don't know about better discharge alternatives.

But in many cases "bad paper" discharges are forced on GIs who don't want to be discharged at all or who don't want to be discharged for the reason or with the character of discharge proposed.

All too often soldiers with PTSD or depression, or with neurological or other physical problems, are misdiagnosed with personality disorders and receive administrative discharges that don't guarantee medical benefits. Unlike all other medical conditions, "personality disorder" is the name of a separate discharge, so the diagnosis appears on veterans' discharge documents.

Many other soldiers with medical or psychiatric problems are wrongly discharged for misconduct as a result of their medical conditions. When medical conditions are not found and treated quickly, soldiers may develop real performance and conduct problems, which commands interpret as misconduct. Under the military's regulations, misconduct warranting an other than honorable discharge or court-martial takes precedence over medical proceedings. Even when PTSD or other illness or injury is recognized, it is considered a collateral problem rather than the cause of the AWOL, drug use, or other "misconduct."

Legal assistance and independent medical examinations are frequently required to prevent these discharges or to challenge them later through the military's discharge review system. Veterans can apply for upgrades of less than honorable discharges, and changes in the reasons for discharge, through each service's Discharge Review Board. The Boards for Correction of Military (or Naval) Records can change discharges to or from medical discharge or retirement. Although success rates before these boards are not high, good advocacy and documentation can often undo the effects of stigmatizing discharges and ensure important veterans' benefits.

A History of Discharge Counseling

Many GIs during the Vietnam War wanted or needed to get out of the service, and many were forced out with other than honorable discharges as a result of medical problems. Although the names of discharge are slightly different, most of the discharges are the same or similar today. Vietnam-era commands frequently claimed discharges were impossible, ignoring or losing applications and dismissing problems that warranted discharge to maintain troop strength.

But persistent GIs found help from a network of civilian counselors and attorneys, many of them working with coffeehouses and GI movement centers. Counseling centers sprang up all over the country. Some lived on private donations and grants from progressive foundations. Some were supported by churches or national social action organizations. Others simply operated on a shoestring. Local groups created national networks, and national organizations helped their local chapters or offices set up counseling projects. Volunteers all over the country were trained in discharge counseling; some were students, some volunteered through church groups, and some were veterans who knew what they had needed as soldiers. Many counselors in the large antidraft network added military counseling to their work.

The organizations created networks and support structures; groups also grew out of political and community networks involved in other work. The American Friends Service Committee, a Quaker-based organization, trained counselors in some of its local offices. The United States Servicemen's Fund and its progeny, two Support Our Soldiers offices, raised funds for coffeehouses and organizing centers that routinely offered military counseling as part of their work. The National Lawyers Guild set up Military Law Project offices in Asia and trained many of its own members around the country to practice military law. Groups on the West Coast and in Asia formed the Pacific Counseling Service, which had its own fund-raising and support office. Some of these groups were precursors of the organizations that established the GI Rights Network and its hotline after the first Gulf war.

Some counselors and groups approached the work with intentional neutrality, offering help to soldiers because of the huge need. But a great many of these volunteers engaged in both activism and discharge counseling. The Center for Servicemen's Rights (CSR) in San Diego had a collective of volunteers that included active duty sailors, a few Marines, veterans, and civilian activists. Some of the veteran members had first come to CSR for help with a discharge, or wrote articles for its newspaper, *Up from the Bottom*.

The counseling movement grew and organized itself, training new counselors and developing counseling manuals and pamphlets for GIs. The Central Committee for Conscientious Objectors (CCCO) created an invaluable manual, called simply the *Military Counseling Manual*, with regular updates. One local gay center developed a legal counseling manual on gay discharges. The first of its kind, the manual was copied and used all over the country. Little mimeographed newsletters for counselors covered changes in regulations and court cases. The National Lawyers Guild and other leftist legal groups wrote training manuals for military law attorneys. As GIs became counselors and counselors learned from GIs, their work and training materials expanded to cover redress of grievance procedures and other GI rights issues.

The period also saw some incredible resources for GIs, including CCCO's *Advice for Conscientious Objectors in the Armed Forces*, their little *Getting Out* booklet, and a series of pamphlets on individual discharges. Leaflets and pamphlets on nonjudicial punishment and discharge upgrades made their way around bases. The GI rights book *Turning the Regs Around*, with information on dissent, discharges, and legal rights, was distributed throughout the country and sent to GIs and coffeehouses in Asia.

This network helped many thousands of GIs to get out of the military and along the way trained GI activists to know their rights. Counselors assisted GI activists to arm themselves with important legal knowledge and sometimes helped them leave the military legally in the face of command hostility about antiwar protests. Many GIs who came to counseling centers for assistance with individual problems stayed to become involved in counseling or became involved in antiwar work taking place on the other side of the office. Kathleen Gilberd, involved in both efforts, found that GIs often ended up "politicizing" the counselors and taught them new reasons to oppose the war.

Many GIs' discharge requests were turned down or simply ignored, and many other GIs were too angry or troubled to go through several months of a discharge process. AWOL and unauthorized absence (UA, the equivalent term in the Navy and Marine Corps) rates soared during the war, not only as a matter of resistance but also through soldiers who just needed to go home. Canada, whose government treated U.S. military resisters humanely, became home for a generation of refugees and resisters.

In the aftermath of the war, public opinion shifted, and veterans organizations pressed for amnesty for deserters living abroad. Two amnesty programs allowed many to return, with blemished records but without punishment. Deserters from the Vietnam era still return from Canada or resurface after years of living quietly in the United States. These cases are now an embarrassment for the Army and Marine Corps in particular, and some Vietnam-era resisters have received quick other than honorable discharges with relatively little fuss in the past few years. But each of the deserters ran the risk, for many years, that the military would end their civilian life and punish them with federal convictions, prison time, and bad conduct or dishonorable discharges.

The GI counseling movement of the Vietnam era provided a foundation for today's national GI Rights Network and other counseling organizations. Some of the impetus and practical experience with military law came from attorneys and counselors who had rendered draft and military counseling 30 years before; among them were military law attorneys who began their practices with the NLG's Military Law Project offices in Japan, Okinawa, and the Philippines, and long-time activist members of Vietnam Veterans Against the War. Several national and regional counseling centers continued their work after the Vietnam War, helping soldiers with CO claims and other discharges. The Military Law Project morphed into the Guild's Military Law Task Force in the mid-1970s, expanding its work to other areas of military law and to veterans law.

Although some of those groups and individuals continued military law and counseling in the intervening years, others got involved again during the first Gulf war, along with a number of new activists who became counselors. Shortly after the Gulf war, these "veterans" of the GI counseling movement and some of the veterans who served during the war held a series of meetings and a retreat to share counseling experiences from the war. They formed the GI Rights Network and set up its toll-free hotline for GI counseling in the early 1990s.

As new tech-savvy members joined, and some old hands worked to catch up on the technology, the network added an informative Web site and then e-mail counseling. Internet and cell phone networks made it possible to work with GIs in isolated areas and often in combat zones. After 9/11 the network gained a new generation of veterans, family members of soldiers serving in Iraq or Afghanistan, and other supporters.

Now over 20 groups strong, the network has counseling centers working with service members at (among other places) Fort Bragg and Camp Lejeune in North Carolina, Camp Pendleton in Southern California, the complex of naval and Marine bases in San Diego, Fort Lewis and Naval Station Bremerton in Washington, Fort Richardson in Alaska, Fort Hood and Lackland Air Force Base in Texas, as well as in New York City, Philadelphia, San Francisco, Oakland, and Bammental, Germany. In 2008 new groups in Oklahoma City and Albuquerque joined the network. New counselors are training in the Midwest and the South.

Iraq Veterans Against the War, Veterans for Peace, and Vietnam Veterans Against the War provide support and a source of new counselors. In some areas local peace centers donate office space and provide financial sponsorship. Network policy is nondirective: counselors never ask for political or moral agreement from callers and clients, and they make a point of providing information and choices rather than advice and decisions. Fundamental to the network is the idea of empowering GIs to make their own decisions in the face of an institution that would deny them choices.

Although the network counselors are diligent in not pushing their political views on GIs, many GIs become involved in protest activity at the same time they are getting legal support, empowered in part by information about the regulations that protect them and the knowledge that counselors and attorneys are available if they face reprisals. IVAW and antiwar activists make sure that soldiers know how to find counseling, and invite network groups to bring information to their events. And in many cases the process of discharge is radicalizing. Soldiers with pressing reasons to go home often find they are suddenly labeled troublemakers or cowards, getting harassment instead of help from their superiors. Many soldiers who otherwise support the military's objectives rethink their views as they consider how the military treats its own in difficult circumstances.

The network estimates that it helped over 40,000 soldiers through its hotline in 2007, and many more who gathered discharge information from the Web site or e-mail discussion with counselors. That number represents only a fraction of the GIs who get information from their buddies or are quietly given GI Rights Network handouts by chaplains or military doctors.

This counseling movement is in it for the long haul. Its experience is a reminder that ending a war does not mean ending all illegal and immoral wars. It teaches us that the military is consistent in its willingness to treat its own members like expendable weapons, offering little help, treatment, or benefits when GIs are harmed, not only by the war but by the war's stresses on the conditions of military life. But it also teaches us that as long as these problems continue, GIs, veterans, and their civilian supporters will help one another with support and information to get out, to resist, and to disengage.

NINE

The Families

THE VICTIMS OF THE IRAQ AND AFGHANISTAN WARS include not just the soldiers on both sides and the hundreds of thousands of civilians who have been killed and maimed. They are also the families of our troops—the spouses, mothers, fathers, brothers, sisters, life partners, grandparents, in-laws, cousins, nieces, nephews, aunts, and uncles—who are victimized by these wars. Almost everyone knows someone who has been directly affected. Families must cope with fear during deployments, the possibility of the knock on the door that means news of death, and all too often they must cope with injuries that result in the loss of their loved ones as they once knew them. This impact persists both during the war and when the soldiers return home as their families deal with serious injuries, including brain damage, post-traumatic stress disorder, and suicide.

Families bear a heavier burden in the Iraq and Afghanistan wars than in past conflicts because of the multiple deployments our troops face today. Many soldiers are deployed two, three, or even four times for combat stints of 12 or 15 months. Redeployments put a tremendous strain on marriages and children; some families report children with nightmares, bedwetting, and heartache. A 2007 study funded by the Pentagon found that abuse and neglect by mothers can rise when fathers are deployed and redeployed.[1]

The caseload of the Miles Foundation, which provides assistance to military wives who are victims of domestic violence, has more than quadrupled during the Afghan and Iraq wars. While the government affords inadequate medical care to returning soldiers, it also falls short of providing sufficient support for spouses and children of absent, wounded, and traumatized troops.

Just as the Bush administration minimized civilian casualties by calling them "collateral damage," so it discounted the suffering of military families. One thing the government learned from the Vietnam War is that the American people get upset when they see the caskets of their fallen soldiers. As a result the Department of Defense has assiduously tried to hide the returning war dead from public view. Sixty-three percent of families with soldiers killed in the war favor media coverage of their funerals. Yet the Pentagon has refused to allow coverage. Gina Gray was fired as public affairs director at Arlington National Cemetery after she challenged a new policy that moved the media area even farther from the funerals, effectively preventing the taking of photographs and making the services inaudible.[2] As we went to press, the Pentagon, responding to pressure, decided to allow photographs of flag-draped caskets at Dover Air Force Base if the families of the fallen troops wish.

A mother who called herself "Gold Star Mom" wrote on the *Washington Post* blog that her request for a photograph of her son's body "being treated with dignity and respect" as he arrived at Dover Air Force Base was repeatedly denied. The reason given: photographing was "against Army regulations," which, she was told, aimed "to protect the privacy of the families." The Defense Department strongly discourages family members from coming to Dover to watch the unloading of caskets. "America should be privileged to witness the ceremony and dignity of a military funeral," Gold Star Mom observed. "America should be required to witness and experience a family's mournful loss as they bury their loved one, whose years on this earth were too few. America should be allowed to mourn, if only briefly, as they bear witness to the human cost of war. America owes at least that much respect for those who died."[3]

In this chapter we relate the stories of a number of family members who have decided to take action against the wars in Iraq and Afghanistan, a phenomenon that is much stronger than the family movement of the Vietnam era. The chapter also examines the important role of families in countering recruiter lies and misconduct, as discussed in Chapter 8. Because families are seldom bound by military rules, they have greater freedom to act; as a result this chapter does not need discussion of military law and regulations. Instead, it focuses on the work of the family organizations as examples for others who may wish to speak out.

Gold Star Families for Peace

President Woodrow Wilson coined the term *gold star mother* in 1918 to signify the supreme sacrifice made by fallen soldiers and to give their families a sense of consolation and pride. Wilson recommended that American women wear black arm bands adorned with a gold star to represent a family member who had died serving his or her country. During the Vietnam War, gold star mothers began speaking out and questioning the war.

In response to the Iraq war, Cindy Sheehan and other parents of fallen soldiers founded Gold Star Families for Peace. "When a mom has a child killed in a war, she becomes a Gold Star Mom," Sheehan said. "We expanded the idea to include all family members because an entire family is affected because of the death. Our group includes every type of relative to a soldier."[4]

In August 2005, a year after her son, Spec. Casey Sheehan, was killed while serving with the Army in Iraq, Sheehan established Camp Casey down the road from George W. Bush's Crawford, Texas, ranch, where the president was on a five-week vacation. Sheehan waited unavailingly for Bush to answer her question: "What noble cause did my son die for?" She said, "I was told my son was killed in the war on terror. He was killed by George Bush's war of terror on the world."[5] Sheehan's protest started as a small gathering and mushroomed into a demonstration of several thousand people in Crawford and tens of thousands more at solidarity vigils throughout the country.

Bill Mitchell's son Mike was killed in Iraq in the same battle as Casey Sheehan. Mitchell, another founder of Gold Star Families for Peace, was in Crawford with Sheehan. "My life's been devastated," Mitchell told the editor of the *Lone Star Iconoclast*. "It's been turned upside down. Very few aspects of my life have a similarity to the past. It just kind of churns you up, shakes you out, and drops you off. I'm doing much better than I have been. The death of any child is a devastating event for a parent. A piece of your heart dies when your child dies. So I just want to stop this. I don't want to hear about anybody else dying, American or Iraqi."[6]

Sheehan always carries Casey's baby picture with her and passes it around when she gives speeches. She visits the Defense Department's Web site each morning to see who else died in Bush's war while she was sleeping. "And that rips my heart open, because I know there is another mother whose life is going to be ruined that day. So we can't even begin to heal. Why should I want one more mother to go through what I've gone through, because my son is dead . . . The only way [President Bush] can honor my son's sacrifice is to bring the rest of the troops home—to make my son's death count for peace and love, and not war and hatred like he stands for."[7]

When asked for a Memorial Day message from Gold Star Families for Peace in 2005, Sheehan replied: "Honor our children's and our families' sacrifices by bringing the troops home as soon as humanly possible. Honor our men and women in the armed forces by using them only when America is threatened, not to invade countries that pose no threat to the USA. Honor the vets who have served America by meeting their every need. Honor the families of needlessly slain children by realizing that America is a country at war. Look in your hearts, look at the truth about this immoral war, and work for peace. Our children died for peace; make it so."[8]

Military Families Speak Out

Many members of Military Families Speak Out (MFSO) also came to Camp Casey. The largest of the organizations of military families that formed in response to the Iraq war, MFSO's logo entwines a yellow support-the-troops ribbon with a peace symbol. With over 3,600 families and chapters in 29 states and the District of Columbia, MFSO is a diverse group. "The only thing you have to do to join MFSO is to be against this war and you have to have a loved one or relative in the military," says Charley Richardson, who founded the group with his wife, Nancy Lessin, in September 2002 in the run-up to the Iraq war.[9] MFSO's motto is "Support Our Troops. Bring Them Home Now! And Take Care of Them When They Get Here."

People in MFSO have family members going on their second, third, fourth, and fifth deployments. Besides providing support for one another, MFSO members lobby Congress and demonstrate against the war.

Some MFSO members protested the Vietnam War years ago; others never spoke out before joining the organization. Those with sons and daughters in combat share the same fear: the knock on the door from the military representative with the unspeakable news. "For those of us who believe that this war is illegal, it's immoral, it's unjust, it's unjustified, it's wrong, it should never have happened, to have our loved ones over there disrupts our lives in ways that are not comprehended by anyone else who hasn't been in our shoes," Lessin explained.[10]

After Marjorie Cohn gave a lecture about the illegality of the war at the University of California at San Diego in 2008, a man came up and handed her a book. His name was Tim Kahlor, and his son Ryan had suffered serious brain damage in his second tour of duty in Iraq with the Army. "I keep thinking about those families," he said. "It's not just the one soldier; it's a huge ripple effect, whole families destroyed." Kahlor is one of 27 members of MFSO profiled in that book, *For Love of a Soldier—Interviews with Military Families Taking Action against the Iraq War*.[11] We feature some of their stories here.

Mothers and grandmothers like Linda Waste, whose three sons and two grandchildren are all veterans of the Iraq war, understand what families go through: "You hear about a death in your son's unit, wait for seventy-two hours to hear. Then you're so grateful it's not yours. Then you cry from gratitude and grief—gratitude it's not yours, grief for the families who lost theirs." Anne Chay, whose son John was in Iraq, also wondered "who is it going to be today. But even when it's not him, it's not much of a moral victory. It's 22 a week now. Twenty-two other families—brothers, sisters, mothers, fathers—are getting the news. Whether it's me or somebody else, what difference does it make?" Waste also empathizes with Iraqi women who live with the same pain. "How can you possibly believe that an Iraqi woman's life is any less important than mine, that her son's or husband's life is any less important than my son's or husband's?"

"The biggest single issue for those of us lucky enough to get our loved ones home is post-traumatic stress disorder," Lessin notes in the book. "It helps me to help others," says Laura Kent, whose only child committed suicide after suffering with PTSD. Speaking out "is a very important means of therapy" for Melida Arredondo, whose dear stepson was killed in Iraq. "All Marines say they don't leave their friends behind. That's what we're [MFSO] doing. We're not leaving them behind." Her husband Carlos was so grief-stricken when he heard the terrible news from the Marine representatives that he jumped into their van and set it on fire, suffering second and third degree burns in the process. After pressure from many who called and wrote in, the Hollywood police decided not to prosecute Carlos.

Many moms and dads report that when their sons and daughters return from the war, the former soldiers become uncommunicative, haunted by what they saw and did. Many develop PTSD. And some of the parents fall into depression. "I went into such a deep depression," Sarah Tyler said in the book, "I could hardly stand it." Her son Ben, an Army combat photojournalist, served two tours in Iraq. Like so many other Iraq war vets, he won't talk to his mother about the war.

When, in spite of severe scoliosis, her daughter Shanell was deployed to Iraq, Denise Thomas tried to kill herself, believing that would force the Army to send Shanell home. Thomas was furious when she saw Bush's "Mission Accomplished" speech while "Shanell was seeing dead bodies lying in the streets for days, Iraqi women being raped, because there was no local law enforcement." Shanell, who came home with PTSD, is still in the Army Reserve. "If they threaten to send her back," Thomas said, she won't sit quietly: "[I'll] tell everyone how medically-unfit soldiers are treated. It doesn't frighten me anymore. I've learned how to fight back."

All four of Larry Syverson's sons have served in the U.S. military. He began protesting the war before it began and has logged

218 demonstrations. When son Bryce's tour in Iraq was extended, Syverson's wife "broke down at work, crying uncontrollably." Her antidepressant was doubled, and she began seeing a psychiatrist and eventually retired. Syverson started taking blood pressure medication after his sons went to Iraq.

Sarah Fuhro has been politically active in left-wing causes for most of her life. Her son joined the reserves before 9/11 and was later sent to Iraq. In the book Fuhro said she "had no idea how bad it was going to be. I always say MFSO saved me." At one point she came close to having a nervous breakdown. A lot of Fuhro's energy went into her MFSO work. "I'd constantly be meeting other parents in much worse situations: either their child was dead, or their child was there for the fourth or fifth time, or their child was wounded," Fuhro said. "I came to have so much admiration for these people, many of whom are from the military or support the military . . . In a sense, when I do MFSO work, I'm working along with my son, because I'm with the families of other people who were there. We've been tremendous support for each other." Fuhro got arrested the first day of the war for joining a group that entered an Army base without permission in an antiwar protest.

Pat Alviso, whose son Beto has been to Iraq twice, was arrested in a protest in front of the White House with Cindy Sheehan and others. The arrestees refused to pay their fine for "protesting without a permit" and raised a Nuremberg defense. After she returned home to Orange County, California, Alviso started an MFSO chapter.

When Phillip, Laura Kent's only child, came back from Iraq, he was not in the same shape as he was when he left. He was diagnosed with bipolar disorder, "but he had PTSD," his mother said in the book. Phillip shot and killed himself. "I wanted my life to be over for a long time. Now I just thank God that I had him. He was a good son. I have such a hole in my heart right now. But what I'm doing now is important for him. I've been asked to speak at two peace rallies and told everybody his story, how he loved his country and wanted to serve so badly, and how shabbily he was treated when he got home. Whenever I hear about somebody else dying in Iraq, it just breaks my heart. But I've gotten to the point where I can help other families. It helps me to help others."

Stacy Hafley became homeless when her husband Joe was running convoys in Iraq. She described the scene as she went to see him off. "It was the most sickening thing. We had a lot of young wives and pregnant wives. The wives were a wreck. The mothers were hysterical. Some guys were crying when they boarded the bus for the airport. Some guys were throwing up, they were so stressed. One little boy held on to his mom's leg—she was being deployed. He had to be physically pulled off, screaming and crying." Hafley, whose husband has been diagnosed with severe depression and PTSD, "dove headfirst into [MFSO]. It's the best therapy ever. It gave me a goal to work towards, helping other families."

Gilda Carbonaro's only child, Alessandro, was killed in Iraq. "Part of my healing is to do what I can to help the American people understand what a mistake they made, that we are responsible for the deaths of all these people," she said. "This country must come to terms with what was done in our name. I will make this my life's work if need be," she pledged in the interview. "This is how I will honor my son and keep his memory alive."

These courageous families, who endure unspeakable suffering and then join together to support one another and work to the end the war, are tributes to the power of collective action.

Guerrero Azteca Peace Project

Fernando Suarez del Solar was a native of Mexico who spoke little English. The death of his son, Lance Corporal Jesus Alberto Suarez del Solar Navarro, on March 27, 2003, marked the beginning of his activism. He learned English and speaks frequently, traveling throughout most of the United States and to 11 foreign countries, including Iraq, where, he said, "I stood on the very spot where my son died, and was able to bury my hands in the dirt covered with his dried blood, bringing it home with me."[12]

Suarez del Solar founded Guerrero Azteca Peace Project (at azteccapp.netrootz.com) in San Diego. Its mission is to aid families who lose a loved one in the military or other armed conflict with moral support and possibly economic support to help them cope with the loss of a family member; the group also helps people find alternative opportunities to military service, including scholarships. The group's mission includes working for peace internationally and instilling pride and respect for Latino communities and their cultural heritage. Members of Guerrero Azteca do counter-recruitment work and make presentations and organize conferences, with assistance from Latino activists, to help youth consider peace and higher education as their goals.

Another project Suarez del Solar developed is the planting of a tree for each fallen soldier in the Escondido, California, park where Jesus loved to spend time. Enlisting the city of Escondido to help with the effort, Suarez del Solar has created a lasting tribute to those who sacrificed their lives in Iraq.

September Eleventh Families for Peaceful Tomorrows

Another group of families who joined together to honor their lost loved ones by working for peace is September Eleventh Families for Peaceful Tomorrows. It was founded by family members of those killed on September 11 who have united to turn their grief into action for peace. By developing and advocating nonviolent options and actions in the pursuit of justice, they hope to break the cycle of violence engendered by war and terrorism. Acknowledging their common experience with all people affected by violence throughout the world, they work to create a safer and more peaceful world for everyone.

Their Web site, PeacefulTomorrows.org, lists their unifying principles: to promote dialogue on alternatives to war while educating and raising the public consciousness on issues of war, peace, and the underlying causes of terrorism; to support and offer fellowship to others seeking nonviolent responses to all forms of terrorism, both individual and institutional; to call attention to threats to civil liberties, human rights, and other freedoms in the United States as a consequence of war; to acknowledge their fellowship with all people affected by violence and war, recognizing that the resulting deaths are overwhelmingly civilian; to encourage a multilateral, collaborative effort to bring those responsible for the September 11, 2001, attacks to justice in accordance with the principles of international law; to promote a U.S. foreign policy that places a priority on internationally recognized principles of human rights, democracy, and self-rule; and to demand ongoing investigations into the events leading up to the September 11 attacks, including exhaustive examinations of U.S. foreign policy and national security failures.

David Potorti, codirector of September Eleventh Families for Peaceful Tomorrows, moved by Cindy Sheehan's protest, cited the parallels: "The humanity of our families was invisible to the people who murdered them on September 11th. The humanity of Afghan civilians, already suffering, was invisible to the Americans who supported the bombing of their country. The humanity of Iraqi civilians, already suffering, was invisible to the Americans whipped into war on a series of calculated lies. The humanity of the troops and reservists doing hard time in Iraq is invisible to the people sending them there. And the humanity of those troops killed or maimed for the rest of their lives remains largely invisible to the American people."[13]

Shortly after this country began bombing Afghanistan, people whose family members were killed in the 9/11 attacks went to Afghanistan to share their common grief with families who had lost loved ones in the U.S. bombing there. Derrill Bodley's 20-year-old daughter was on a plane, coming to visit him on September 11. Her plane crashed, and she never arrived to visit her father. Abe Zelmanowitz, 70-year-old Rita Lasar's brother, refused to leave the World Trade Center when he had the chance on September 11; instead, he stayed with his trapped quadriplegic friend. Lasar never saw her brother again.

Shortly after 9/11 Lasar realized that "my government was going to use my brother as a justification for killing other people. And that has a tremendous impact on me. I didn't want that to happen, not in my brother's name." Lasar, speaking on *Democracy Now!* to an Afghani woman whose family members were killed by U.S. bombs, said, "There's no difference between us. My family member died. I'm grieving. And her family—God, I don't know how you survived, just hearing about yours. But you're—we're the same people." Lasar decided to go to Afghanistan "to see the people who have been left behind while their families died."[14]

Parents: Biggest Obstacle to Military Recruiters

The military has recognized parents as a major obstacle to recruitment, realizing that their refusal to allow their children to be used as cannon fodder is a major impediment. Many parents are afraid that their children will have to fight and kill or be killed in a war they do not support. Some complain that recruiters hand out "things that the parents did not want in their homes, including very violent video games."[15]

Parents are targeted with a special series of advertisements. The Army's Web site devotes a section (at http://www.goarmy.com/for_parents/index.jsp) to parents. The site touts the value of the military's training in law enforcement, engineering, law, and medicine, as well as the money it provides for college. It tells families, "You made them strong. We'll make them Army strong." The whole campaign urges parents to listen to their children's reasons (the recruiters' promises kids believed) and "stand by them" as they pursue their dreams. Parents have to click to a separate subsection on deployment before they see any reference to danger or combat. Once there, they are assured that some deployed soldiers go to Hawaii, Italy, Germany, and South Korea, and that those who do step into risky areas have every attention paid to their safety.

The Army has also launched campaigns to increase the ranks of Latino recruits. Commercials in English and Spanish minimize the dangers of being in the military. One of the main targets of this recruitment is mothers. Victoria Varela, chief executive of Cartel Creativo of San Antonio, the advertising agency that created the ads that feature actual Latino recruits, noted that "we've got to put as much emphasis on the mothers as we do on the potential recruits." The campaign has borne fruit. Whereas Latinos signed 10.7 percent of new Army enlistment contracts in 2000, that level increased to nearly 13 percent by the middle of 2002.[16]

A Web site called LeaveMyChildAlone.org counsels parents on the rights they and their children have. It explains how to opt out of the No Child Left Behind database provision that requires schools to provide the military with students' contact information. A recruiter in Ohio pegged it: "Parents are the biggest hurdle we face."[17] "The parents of the kids being sought by recruiters to fight this unpopular war," wrote the *New York Times'* Bob Herbert, "are creating a highly vocal and potentially very effective antiwar movement. In effect, they're saying to their own children: hell no, you won't go."[18]

In 2008 a Marine recruit's mother worked with her son to obtain a discharge during basic training, with assistance from Kathleen Gilberd. He was isolated and intimidated by drill instructors' constant threats. "Suck it up," they told him. "Discharge isn't possible. It would prove you aren't a man. Your parents will hide in shame if you go home now." From that moment, the recruit later told his mom, he knew that everything else they told him was a lie, because that statement was a lie. His parents kept telling him they supported his decision and stood with him all through the discharge process.

Families are a powerful force in the effort to end these wars. They can tell the truth to counter recruiters' deceptions. Families can speak out against war on behalf of their soldiers and veterans, and on their own behalf, as people who are also injured by the wars. They are in a strong position to reach out to other families and their communities with an antiwar message. And they can provide essential support to GIs caught in the military who need to know they are not alone.

· TEN ·

Conclusion

LIKE SOLDIERS DURING the Vietnam War, GIs today ask themselves whether and how to disengage. They find themselves required to weigh the legality and propriety of the Iraq and Afghanistan wars. They ask why they face conditions far beyond the normal problems expected in a military life—shoddy and unsafe equipment, inadequate gear, a broken medical system, commands that ignore serious family hardships, and dehumanization and bigotry in training and in the field. Both the mission and the conditions of the military increasingly cause GIs to disengage from the wars in Iraq and Afghanistan, and often from the military altogether.

Questions of Law and Morality

U.S. military involvement in both of those conflicts violates the Charter of the United Nations, which is part of American law. Lt. Ehren Watada, the first commissioned officer to publicly refuse orders to fight in Iraq, decided, "The war in Iraq is in fact illegal. It is my obligation and my duty to refuse any orders to participate in this war." Raising a Nuremberg defense, Watada concluded, "An order to take part in an illegal war is unlawful in itself. So my obligation is not to follow the order to go to Iraq."[1]

Soldiers, sailors, airmen, and Marines are also struggling with the politics and morality of today's wars. Before he deployed to Iraq, Staff Sergeant Camilo Mejía opposed the Iraq war, but he didn't have the "clarity to openly express [his] doubts about participating in a war [he] believed was unjustified." Mejía "didn't want to be labeled a coward" and he knew that "openly expressing [his] reservations could be construed as unpatriotic and treasonous."[2] While serving in Iraq, Mejía's beliefs crystallized, and he realized he was a conscientious objector.

Many GIs, both men and women, are examining the morality of the wars in Iraq and Afghanistan. "Women are coming back from Iraq without limbs," said Wendy McClinton, an Army veteran and executive vice president of Black Veterans for Social Justice. "How do I hold the child that I left when I don't have arms?"[3] Mejía and McClinton find honor in resistance to an immoral military system.

Joshua Key, a resister living in Canada, said, "I never would have signed up if I'd known I would be blasting into Iraqis' houses, terrorizing women and children, and detaining every man we could find—and all that for $1,200 a month as a private first class. Somehow, somewhere, I would have found a job and a way to survive. I would never have gone to war for my country if I had known what my country was going to do at war in Iraq." Key's advice to youth contemplating enlistment is that "they don't have to live with the moral anguish of fighting an immoral war. It is not true that a soldier's first obligation is to the military. One's first obligation is to the moral truth buried deep inside our own souls. Every person knows what is right and wrong. And we have a duty to live up to it, regardless of what our leaders sometimes say."[4]

Stan Goff, a 26-year Army veteran and member of the Bring Them Home Now! coordinating committee, concurs. In an open letter to GIs in Iraq, Goff wrote that "you are never under any obligation to hate Iraqis" or "to give yourself over to racism and nihilism and the thirst to kill for the sake of killing" or "to let them drive out the last vestige of your capacity to see and tell the truth to yourself and to the world. You do not owe them your souls."[5]

The "Right War" Is Also Wrong

GIs are being sent to Afghanistan in increasing numbers. June 2008 saw more combat deaths in Afghanistan than in Iraq. In light of stepped-up violence in Afghanistan, and for political reasons, George W. Bush moved troops from Iraq to Afghanistan, and President Barack Obama is increasing the troop levels in Afghanistan as well. Although the U.S. invasion of Afghanistan was as illegal as the invasion of Iraq, many Americans see it as a justifiable response to the attacks of September 11, 2001, and the total casualties in that war have been lower than those in Iraq—so far. Few in the United States are currently questioning the legality or propriety of U.S. military involvement in Afghanistan. A July 2008 cover of *Time* magazine called it "The Right War."

Those who conspired to hijack airplanes and kill thousands of people on September 11 are guilty of crimes against humanity. They must be identified and brought to justice in accordance with the law. But retaliation by armed force in Afghanistan is not the answer and will only lead to the deaths of more of our troops and Afghanis.

The hatred that inspired 19 people to blow themselves up and take 3,000 innocents with them has its genesis in a history of U.S. exploitation of people in oil-rich nations around the world. Bush accused the terrorists of targeting our freedom and democracy. But it was not the Statue of Liberty that was destroyed. It was the World Trade Center, symbol of the U.S.-led global economic system, and the Pentagon, heart of the U.S. military, that took the hits. Those who committed these heinous crimes were attacking American foreign policy. That policy resulted in the deaths of one million Iraqis from President Bill Clinton's punishing sanctions. It also led to uncritical support of Israel's brutal occupation of Palestinian lands and the maintenance of more than 700 U.S. military bases in foreign countries.

Conspicuously absent from the national discourse is a political analysis of why the tragedy of 9/11 occurred and a comprehensive strategy to overhaul U.S. foreign policy to address the real reasons for the wrath of those who despise American imperialism. The "global war on terror" has been uncritically accepted by most people in this country. But terrorism is a tactic, not an enemy. You cannot declare war on a tactic. The way to combat terrorism is by identifying and targeting its root causes, including poverty and foreign occupation.

The RAND Corporation released a report on July 29, 2008, that argues, "Current U.S. strategy against the terrorist group al Qaida has not been successful in significantly undermining the group's capabilities." According to RAND, the United States should pursue a counterterrorism strategy against al-Qaeda that emphasizes policing and intelligence gathering rather than a "war on terrorism" approach that relies heavily on military force.[6]

The use of military force in Iran would also be illegal. The UN Charter forbids any country to use, or threaten to use, military force against another country except in self-defense or when the Security Council has given its blessing. In spite of the International Atomic Energy Agency's conclusion of a lack of evidence that Iran is developing nuclear weapons, the Bush White House, Congress, and Israel continued to threaten action against Iran. Nevertheless, in 2008 the antiwar movement fended off passage of a congressional resolution in the House of Representatives that was tantamount to a call for a naval blockade against Iran—considered an act of war under international law. Credit goes to United for Peace and Justice, Code Pink, Peace Action, and dozens of other organizations that pressured Congress to think twice before taking that dangerous step.

As long as U.S. leaders pursue a strategy of global war or total war, they will continue to find new targets for invasion and occupation, and new countries will come along where GIs must ask the same questions. Soldiers are forced to decide whether to continue to serve in those illegal conflicts or to challenge them. They must also must weigh, in accordance with their own beliefs, the morality of those wars and the way they are being conducted. When GIs are given conflicting rules of engagement that often instruct them to shoot at anything that moves, they are put in the position of killing large numbers of civilians and committing war crimes. As those who testified at Winter Soldier confirmed, the atrocities they were forced to commit have taken a large toll on many of them, who carry with them PTSD and heartache.

Mission and Condition

As a result of the crisis in personnel, the military's pressure on soldiers is causing increased difficulties. These difficulties can be seen most clearly in medical problems as troops are pushed beyond their endurance. Serious injuries and illnesses are ignored or underdiagnosed in the rush to deploy and redeploy combat and support troops. Dehumanization and bigotry, most often in the form of racism, sexism, and homophobia, are applied heavily in training and motivation of uncooperative recruits and troops. This bigotry in turn heightens the military's internal dilemma as frustrated GIs take out their anger and pain on people of color, lesbians and gay men, women, and others whom the military has taught them are less than human. Marciela Guzman, a Latina Navy veteran who is now a counter-recruitment activist, says it well: "You're going to this environment thinking you're going to make all this money, but you're going back to a system that is going to keep you down."[7]

For many GIs and families, the starting point of disengagement is not a war but rather its effects on their lives and those of their families. When commands refuse requests to see a doctor or ignore medical recommendations or family problems because they need troops on the ground in Iraq or Afghanistan, it is only one step from frustration over those problems to anger at their causes in the wars themselves. By failing to deal with the lives of its own people, the military creates new dissidents and activists among those who might otherwise continue to support the wars—the conditions of military life are affected more than ever by its mission.

"Mission and condition" have broader societal parallels as well—a government committed to illegal wars requires a massive military budget, taking funds critically needed for education, health, and social welfare programs. Refocusing the budget on "bread, not bombs" would help those most severely affected by the current economic crisis, and provide other options for young men and women forced into military service by today's poverty draft.

Disengaging

Having considered these hard questions, GIs, veterans, families, and the general public in growing numbers are deciding to disengage. Because of increasing resistance within the military and the refusal of the people of Iraq and Afghanistan to give up, the military is stretched beyond capacity. It has to use its existing troops longer and more harshly through redeployments without adequate time to rest and recover, stop-loss to prevent expected discharges, call-ups of reserves and the guard, and efforts to squelch dissent.

Resistance and dissent are now manifesting themselves in a

wide variety of ways. Dissent shows up especially on the Internet but also in long-term organizing by GIs in coffeehouses, in underground papers and blogs, in veterans groups like Iraq Veterans Against the War and Veterans for Peace, in family groups, and in anonymous networks of angry soldiers.

The stories in this book show that GIs, veterans, and those around them are a powerful force of resistance that can have a major impact on whether or not the United States is able to carry out these and future wars of aggression. Vietnam demonstrated what happens when soldiers and veterans say no. "The government can continue to ignore antiwar demonstrations and other symbolic forms of protest, but it cannot ignore the fact that without enough soldiers, it is impossible to sustain a large, long-term occupation in a country like Iraq," counter-recruitment activist Rick Jahnkow of Project on Youth and Non-Military Opportunities (YANO) in San Diego said.[8]

GIs and their allies are developing an antiwar strategy combining new forms of dissent and old ones. They are adding fresh energy to the national counter-recruitment movement already active in schools and communities. Iraq war resister Pablo Paredes, a leader in the GI movement, is increasingly turning his work to young people of recruitment age. "From the IVAW Truth in Recruitment Campaign to the Service Women's Action Network," he said, "the GI resistance movement is taking the fight to the schools. Prevention is our weapon of choice."[9]

The GI Movement Today

An event reminiscent of the Vietnam-era GI movement was IVAW's summer 2008 outreach tour of eight military bases across the country, among them Fort Drum, Fort Stewart, Fort Sill, Fort Hood, and Camp Pendleton. The veterans group organized local events in bars, tattoo shops, coffeehouses, and music venues. Local troops and veterans were invited to learn about their rights and receive legal help in navigating the VA system. Local IVAW chapters and allies were trained to sustain organizing at the various bases after the tour passed through. The tour was developed to expose service members to IVAW and to show the troops and veterans that IVAW can offer them concrete support. The result was many new active duty members for the organization.

Another development that evokes memories of the GI movement during the Vietnam War is the opening of the Coffee Strong, a GI coffeehouse near the entrance of the Fort Lewis military base in Washington State, and the planned opening of another coffeehouse in Killeen, Texas, near Fort Hood. Like the Different Drummer in New York State, the Fort Lewis coffeehouse will be a center for supporting GI rights and war resistance in the region, as well as a place for GIs to have coffee, hear music and lectures, watch poetry slams, and get legal help near the base. Coffee Strong has been endorsed by Seattle Veterans for Peace, Citizen Soldier, Sound Nonviolent Opponents of War, Fellowship of Reconciliation, and Physicians for Social Responsibility. Last year, the Seattle chapter of IVAW began publishing *GI Voice*, a publication that makes its way into Fort Lewis, and it has also begun a GI Radio project.[10]

These are the first new GI coffeehouses since the 1970s, when such coffeehouses proliferated throughout the country. Organizers of the Under the Hood coffeehouse in Killeen emphasize their link to the Oleo Strut, the coffeehouse there during the Vietnam War.

A striking difference between the Vietnam era and the current period is Canada's treatment of American military resisters. Whereas tens of thousands of GIs found refuge in Canada during the Vietnam War, U.S. resisters in Canada today—believed to number about 200—face an uphill battle. Canada's House of

Commons took a nonbinding vote on June 3, 2008, to "immediately implement a program to allow conscientious objectors and their immediate family members . . . to apply for permanent resident status and remain in Canada" and called for an immediate halt to planned deportations.[11] But the conservative Canadian government is ignoring the House of Commons' decision and has begun deporting war resisters. The first was Pfc. Robin Long, deported from Canada in July 2008 and handed over to U.S. military authorities. In August 2008 Long was convicted of desertion and sentenced to 15 months confinement and a dishonorable discharge. However, another resister, Joshua Key, got some good news on July 4, 2008. A Canadian federal court justice overruled a decision by Canada's Immigration and Refugee Board rejecting Key's asylum bid and ordered reconsideration of his case. Justice Robert Barnes ruled that Key had been forced to systematically violate the Geneva Conventions in Iraq and he thus had a legitimate refugee claim.

Thanks to the antiwar movement, two-thirds of the American people oppose the Iraq war. They object to the continued loss of American life occasioned by what the Bush administration misnamed "Operation Iraqi Freedom." President Obama favors, at a minimum, leaving U.S. occupation troops in Iraq indefinitely to train Iraqi security forces and carry out "counterinsurgency operations." That course would not end the occupation. The American people must join the GI movement in calling for bringing home— not redeploying—all U.S. troops and mercenaries, closing the U.S. military bases in Iraq, and relinquishing all efforts to control Iraqi oil. And as more and more troops are sent to Afghanistan— resulting in increased U.S. and Afghan casualties, including a large number of civilians—opposition to that war is growing within the military. Americans must oppose continued U.S. military involvement in that war as well.

The success of the antiwar movement will depend in large part on its ability to make linkages with social and economic issues. As Aimee Allison and David Solnit wrote in their book *Army of None*, "The full potential of a progressive peace and justice movement will only be realized when there is an observable link between efforts to stop war and efforts to address inequality in class, race, ethnicity, immigration status, and other socioeconomic factors that determine who ends up being sacrificed in our government's wars."[12] Jennifer Hogg, who joined the military when she was still in high school, understands this well. "Would the young, the poor, the single mothers feel their only option was to enlist if adequate housing, jobs and healthcare were available?" she asked.[13] In these desperate economic times, Hogg's question becomes even more significant.

Those without apparent alternatives to the military and those in the military who seek to explore their alternatives can choose to disengage. They follow in the honorable footsteps of soldiers and veterans who have forged a path for us all.

Appendix: Resources

GI Rights and Legal Help

GI Rights Network
National Hotline 877-447-4487
From overseas 415-487-2635
From Germany 06223-47506 ˙
girights@girightshotline.org
www.girightshotline.org

Military Law Task Force
of the National Lawyers Guild
730 N. First Street
San Jose, CA 95112
619-463-2369
info@mltf.info
www.nlgmltf.org

Center on Conscience and War
1830 Connecticut Ave., NW
Washington, DC 20009
202-483-2220
www.centeronconscience.org

Servicemembers Legal Defense Network
P.O. Box 65301
Washington, DC 20035
202-328-3244
www.sldn.org
(focusing on the "don't ask, don't tell" policy)

Military Women's Support Groups

Miles Foundation
P.O. Box 423
Newtown, CT 06470
203-270-7861
milesfdn@aol.com

Service Women's Action Network
info@servicewomen.org
http://servicewomen.org

Veterans Rights and Benefits

National Veterans Legal Services Project
P.O. Box 65762
Washington, DC 20035
www.nvlsp.org

National Organization of Veterans Advocates
1425 K Street, NW, Suite 350
Washington, DC 20005
877-483-8238
www.vetadvocates.com

Swords to Plowshares
1060 Howard Street
San Francisco, CA 94103
415-252-4788
www.swords-to-plowshares.org
(working primarily in the San Francisco Bay Area)

Black Veterans for Social Justice
665 Willoughby Avenue
Brooklyn, New York 11206
718-852-6004

Veterans Consortium Pro Bono Program
701 Pennsylvania Ave., NW, Suite 131
Washington, DC 20004
888-838-7727 or 202-628-8164
www.vetsprobono.org
(assistance with cases at the U.S. Court of Appeals for Veterans Claims)

Veterans Activist Organizations

Iraq Veterans Against the War
ivaw@ivaw.org
215-241-7123
www.ivaw.org

Veterans Against the Iraq War
201-876-0430
www.vaiw.org

Veterans for Peace
314-725-6005
vfp@igc.org
www.veteransforpeace.org

Veterans for America
www.veteransforamerica.org
(publishers of the online *American Veterans and Servicemember's Survival Guide*)

Vietnam Veterans Against the War
773-276-4189
www.vvaw.org

Other veterans resource groups can be found in the Appendix of the *American Servicemembers and Veterans Survival Guide*, www.veterans foramerica.org.

Organizations of Military Families

Guerrero Azteca Peace Project
760-746-4568
gaztecaproject@yahoo.com
www.guerreroazteca.org

Military Families Speak Out
617-522-9323
mfso@mfso.org
www.mfso.org

Gold Star Families Speak Out
562-500-9097
www.gsfso.org

September Eleventh Families for Peaceful Tomorrows
212-598-0970
www.peacefultomorrows.org

Military Resistance Organizing and Support Groups

Courage to Resist
510-488-3559
www.couragetoresist.org

Iraq Veterans Against the War
ivaw@ivaw.org
P.O. Box 8296
Philadelphia, PA 19101
215-241-7123
www.ivaw.org

The Military Project
contact@militaryproject.org
www.militaryproject.org
(supports the GI Special online newsletter)

Peace and Justice Groups

United for Peace and Justice Coalition (UFPJ)
212-868-5545
www.unitedforpeace.org

Act Now to Stop War and End Racism (ANSWER)
1247 E Street, SE
Washington, DC 20003
202-544-3389
info@internationalanswer.org
www.internationalanswer.org

Code Pink
www.codepink4peace.org

Grandmothers for Peace
www.grandmothersforpeace.org

Women's International League for Peace and Freedom
www.wilpf.org

American Friends Service Committee
www.afsc.org

National Network Opposing the Militarism of Youth
www.nnomy.org

Notes

Introduction

1. John Kerry, "How Do You Ask a Man to Be the Last Man to Die for a Mistake?" *History News Network*, http://hnn.us/articles/3631 .html, February 17, 2004.

2. See Marjorie Cohn, *Cowboy Republic: Six Ways the Bush Gang Has Defied the Law* (Sausalito, CA: PoliPointPress, 2007), 51–63.

3. Yvonne Latty, *In Conflict—Iraq War Veterans Speak Out on Duty, Loss, and the Fight to Stay Alive* (Sausalito, CA: PoliPointPress, 2006), 25, 31.

4. Office of the Assistant Secretary of Defense for Public Affairs, Magazine and Book Branch, quoted in David Cortright, *Soldiers in Revolt: The American Military Today* (New York: Anchor Press, 1975), 13.

5. Col. Robert D. Heinl Jr., "The Collapse of the Armed Forces," *Armed Forces Journal*, June, 7, 1971, http://chss.montclair.edu/english/ furr/Vietnam/heinl.html.

6. Cortright, *Soldiers in Revolt*, 49.

7. Ibid., 182, 222.

8. Jim Goodman, *Gig Sheet*, quoted in Cortright, *Soldiers in Revolt*.

9. See Jorge Mariscal, "The Poverty Draft," *Sojourners Magazine* 36, no. 6 (2007), 32–35.

10. "The Human Toll," *Navy Times*, February 9, 2009, www.navy times.com.

Chapter 1: Resisting Illegal Wars

1. Record of trial, *United States v. Pablo Paredes*, San Diego, CA, April 6, 2005; May 4, 2005; May 11, 2005; May 12, 2005, pp. 257, 260.

2. Ibid., 217–218.

3. Ibid., 238.

4. Noam Chomsky, *At War with Asia* (Oakland: AK Press, 2005), 164.

5. See Marjorie Cohn, "End the Occupation of Iraq—and Afghanistan," July 30, 2008, http://marjoriecohn.com/2008/07/end-occupation -of-iraq-and-afghanistan_3854.html.

6. Robert N. Strassfeld, "The Vietnam War on Trial: The Court-Martial of Dr. Howard B. Levy," 1994, *Wisconsin Law Review* 839 (1994).

7. Cortright, *Soldiers in Revolt*.

Chapter 2: Modern Conscientious Objectors

1. *United States v. Seeger*, 380 U.S. 163, 169 (1965).

2. DoD Directive 1300.6, "Conscientious Objectors," May 5, 2007; Army Regulation (AR) 600-43, "Conscientious Objection," August 21, 2006; Naval Military Personnel Manual (MILPERSMAN) 1900-020, "Convenience of the Government Separation Based on Conscientious Objection," August 22, 2002; "Marine Corps Order (MCO) 1306.6E, "Conscientious Objection," November 21, 1986; Air Force Instruction (AFI) 36-3204, "Procedures for Applying as a Conscientious Objector," July 15, 1994.

3. Ibid.

4. Camilo Mejía, *Road from Ar Ramadi* (New York: New Press, 2007), 126, 170–171.

5. Ibid., 139.

6. Ibid., 213.

7. Ibid., 223.

8. Ibid., 299.

9. Ibid., 240.

10. Record of trial: *United States v. Mejía-Castillo*.

11. Ibid.

12. Mejía, *Road from Ar Ramadi*, 300.

13. American Civil Liberties Union, "After NYCLU Files Suit, Army Grants Honorable Discharge to Soldier Who Objects to War," press release, May 26, 2006, http://www.aclu.org/natsec/warpowers/ 25721prs20060526.html; Case record, *Martin v. Secretary of the Army*, 463 F.Supp.2d 287 (N.D.N.Y. 2006).

14. Case record, *Hanna v. Secretary of Army*, 513 F.3d 4 (2008).

15. Ibid.

16. Case record, *Janke v. McDonough*, No. 06cv0261 J (S.D. Cal. 2007).

17. Larry Christian, personal communication with authors.

18. Case record, *Zabala v. Hagee*, 2007 WL 963234 (N.D.Cal. 2007).

19. Case record, *Watson v. Geren*, 486 F.Supp.2d 226 (E.D.N.Y. 2007).

20. Ibid.

21. Case record, *Aguayo v. Harvey*, 476 F.3d 971 (2007).

22. Transcript of general court-martial, *United States v. Augustin Aguayo*, March 6, 2007, p. 250.

23. "Refusing to Kill—Katherine Jashinski's Public Statement," Fort Benning, *The Objector: A Magazine of Conscience and Resistance*, November 17, 2005, http://www.objector.org/cground/kjstate.html.

24. "Woman GI Publicly Stands against War as She Faces Immediate Deployment to Middle East," Citizen Soldier, November 17, 2005, www.citizen-soldier.org/katherinejashinski.html.

25. Transcript of court-martial, *United States v. Katherine Jashinski*, May 23, 2006, Fort Benning, GA.

26. Aidan Delgado, *The Sutras of Abu Ghraib: Notes from a Conscientious Objector in Iraq* (Boston: Beacon Press, 2007), 173.

27. Ibid., 78.

28. Ibid., 204.

29. Government Accountability Office, Report to Congressional Committees, "Number of Formally Reported Applications for Conscientious Objectors Is Small Relative to the Total Size of the Armed Forces," GAO-07-1196, September 2007.

30. Ibid., 3.

31. *Seeger*, 380 U.S. 163; *Welsch v. United States*, 389 U.S. 333 (1970).

32. *Seeger*, 380 U.S. 163.

33. *United States v. James*, 417 F.2d 826 (4th Cir. 1969).

34. See, for example, GI Rights Hotline, www.girightshotline.org; Center on Conscience and War, www.centeronconscience.org. See also Robert A. Seeley, *Advice for Conscientious Objectors in the Armed Forces*, 5th ed. (Philadelphia: CCCO, 1998). Beth Ellen Boyle, ed., *Words of Conscience: Religious Statements on Conscientious Objection*, 10th ed. (Washington, DC: CCW, 1983).

Chapter 3: Winter Soldier

1. "1971 Winter Soldier Hearings: Opening Statement by William Crandell, 1st Marine Division," *AlterNet*, March 10, 2008, http://www.alternet.org/story/79137/.

2. "1971 Winter Soldier Hearings, 1st Marine Division Panel," *AlterNet*.

3. Ibid.

4. "Winter Soldier Investigation," *Bamboo Web Dictionary*, http://www.bambooweb.com/articles/W/I/Winter_Soldier_Investigation.html.

5. "Winter Soldier Investigation: Testimony Given in Detroit, Michigan on January 13, 1971, February 1 and 2, 1971," The Sixties Project, http://www2.iath.virginia.edu/sixties/HTML_docs/Resources/Primary/Winter_Soldier/WS_03_1Marine.html.

6. John Kerry, "How Do You Ask a Man to Be the Last Man to Die for a Mistake?" History News Network, http://hnn.us/articles/3631.html, February 17, 2004.

7. Iraq Veterans Against the War and Glantz, *Winter Soldier: Iraq and Afghanistan* (Chicago: Haymarket Books, 2008).

8. Aaron Glantz, "Vets Break Silence on Iraq War Crimes," *IPS News*, http://www.alternet.org/story/78352/, Mar. 7, 2008.

9. Ackerman, "Iraq Veterans to Testify at Their Own 'Winter Soldier.'"

10. Institute for Public Accuracy, "Iraq Veterans Speak. Winter Soldier Hearings," news release, March 12, 2008.

11. Maya Schenwar, "Five Years into War, Soldiers Speak," *Truthout*, March 19, 2008, http://www.truthout.org/article/five-years-into-war-soldiers-speak-0.

12. Dahr Jamail, "Winter Soldiers Sound Off," *Progressive*, April 2008, p. 27.

13. Anna Badkhen, "Veterans Recall Horrors of War in Live Broadcast," *Boston Globe*, March 16, 2008.

14. Penny Coleman, "Winter Soldier: America Must Hear These Iraq Vets' Stories," *AlterNet*, March 15, 2008, http://www.alternet.org/story/797890/.

15. "Winter Soldier: U.S. Vets, Active-Duty Soldiers from Iraq and Afghanistan Testify about the Horrors of War," *DemocracyNow!*, March 17, 2008, http://www.democracynow.org/2008/3/17/winter_soldier_us_vets_active_duty.

16. Badkhen, "Veterans Recall Horrors of War in Live Broadcast."

17. "Winter Soldier: U.S. Vets, Active Duty Soldiers from Iraq and Afghanistan Testify about the Horrors of War," *DemocracyNow!*. March 17, 2008.

18. Jamail, "Winter Soldiers Sound Off," p. 27.

19. Anthony Swofford, "Vet in a Suit: Testimony from the Iraq Veterans Against the War," *Slate*, March 17, 2008, http://www.slate.com/2186755/.

20. "Winter Soldier CON'D: U.S. Vets, Active-Duty Soldiers from Iraq and Afghanistan Testify about the Horrors of War," *DemocracyNow!*, March 18, 2008, http://www.democracynow.org/2008/3/18/winter_soldier_contd_us_vets_active.

21. Ibid.

22. Coleman, "Winter Soldier: America Must Hear These Iraq Vets' Stories."

23. "Half Decade of War: Five Years after Iraq Invasion, Soldiers Testify at Winter Soldier Hearings," *DemocracyNow!*, March 19, 2008, http://www.democracynow.org/2008/3/19/half_a_decade_of_war_five.

24. Ibid.

25. "Winter Soldier CON'D," *DemocracyNow!*, March 18, 2008.

26. Jamail, "Winter Soldiers Sound Off."

27. Wayne Madsen, "Winter Soldier: Evidence of War Crimes Presented," *Rock Creek Free Press*, April 2008, p. 7.

28. Ackerman, "Soldiers Testify at Second Winter Soldier. Veterans from Wars in Iraq and Afghanistan Describe Systematic Brutality."

29. Steve Vogel, "War Stories Echo an Earlier Winter," *Washington Post*, March 15, 2008.

30. Ibid.

31. Madsen, "Winter Soldier: Evidence of War Crimes Presented."

32. Aaron Glantz, "Iraq Veterans Describe Atrocities to Lawmakers," *OneWorld.net*, May 17, 2008, http://us.oneworld.net/article/view/160567/1/.

33. Liliana Segura, "Iraq Vets Testify to War Atrocities, Vow to Fight and Resist Bush Policy," *AlterNet*, May 20, 2008, http://www.alternet.org/story/85725/.

34. Kristofer Shawn Goldsmith, "Testimony of Iraq War Veteran to the U.S. Congress," GlobalResearch.org, May 17, 2008, http://www.globalresearch.ca/index.php?context=va&aid=9012.

35. Ibid.

36. Segura, "Iraq Vets Testify to War Atrocities, Vow to Fight and Resist Bush Policy."

Chapter 4: Dissent and Disengagement

1. Tara McKelvey, "The Officers' War," *American Prospect*, June 3, 2008.

2. Ehren Watada, press conference, Tacoma, Washington, June 7, 2006, quoted in "First Officer Publicly Resists War," MarjorieCohn.com, http://marjoriecohn.com/2006/01/first-officer-publicly-resists-war.html.

3. John Loran Kiel Jr., "When Soldiers Speak Out: A Survey of Provisions Limiting Freedom of Speech in the Military," *Perameters*, Autumn 2007, 69.

4. Marc Cooper, "About Face, The Growing Antiwar Movement in the Military," *Nation*, January 8/15, 2007, 16.

5. "Marines Cut and Run—Drop Charges against Vet Who Claimed Iraq War Is Illegal," *CommonDreams.org News Center*, July 24, 2008, http://www.commondreams.org/news2007/0629-08.htm.

6. Aaron Glantz, "Army 'Rewards' Outspoken Antiwar Soldier," *Inter Press Service*, April 15, 2008, http://www.antiwar.com/glantz/?articleid=12698.

7. *Turning the Regs Around* (San Diego Turning the Regs Around Committee, 1972).

8. 10 U.S.C. sec. 1034.

9. *Parker, Warden et al. v. Levy*, 417 U.S. 733, 758 (1974).

10. *United States v. Wilcox*, 66 M.J. 442, No. 05-0159 (U.S.Ct.App. for Armed Forces, July 15, 2008).

11. Thom Shanker, "Top Ranking Officer Warns U.S. Military to Stay Out of Politics," *International Herald Tribune*, May 25, 2008, http://www.iht.com/articles/2008/05/25/america/pent.php.

Chapter 5: Challenging Racism

1. T. Christian Miller, "Iraq: Prisoner Abuse Appears More Extensive," *Los Angeles Times*, May 2, 2004.

2. Iraq Veterans Against the War and Glantz, *Winter Soldier*, 98.

3. Ibid., 99.

4. Ibid., 99–100.

5. Ibid., 100.

6. Bill W., "Iraq Veterans Against the War: 'Winter Soldier 2008'," *Crooks and Liars*, March 16, 2008, http://www.crooksandliars.com/2008/03/16/iraq-veterans-against-the-war-winter-soldier-2008/.

7. Inigo Gilmore and Teresa Smith, "'If You Start Looking at Them as Humans,' Then How Are You Gonna Kill Them?'" *Guardian (UK)*, March 29, 2006.

8. Iraq Veterans Against the War and Glantz, *Winter Soldier*, 96.

9. Aimee Allison, "You May Face Discrimination," in *10 Excellent Reasons Not to Join the Military*, ed. Elizabeth Weill-Greenberg (New York: New Press, 2006), 104.

10. Delgado, *The Sutras of Abu Ghraib*.

11. Mejía, *Road from Ar Ramadi*.

12. Gilmore and Smith, "'If You Start Looking at Them as Humans.'"

13. Jonathan W. Hutto Sr., *Antiwar Soldier: How to Dissent within the Ranks of the Military* (New York: Nation Books, 2008).

14. Mejía, *Road to Ar Ramadi*, 183–184.

15. Allison, "You May Face Discrimination," 105–106.

16. David Holthouse, "A Few Bad Men," Southern Poverty Law Center, July 7, 2006, http://www.splcenter.org/intel/news/item.jsp?aid-66.

17. "Negroes' Death Toll High in Vietnam," *New York Times*, February 15, 1967.

18. Kief Schladweiler, librarian, *African-American Involvement in the Vietnam War*, http://www.aavw.org/.

19. "Army Aide Urges Race Awareness," *New York Times*, October 14, 1969.

20. House Committee on Armed Forces, *Inquiry into the Disturbances at Marine Corps Base Camp Lejeune, on July 20, 1969*, Wash. DC GPO, 1969, 91st Cong., 1st sess., Dec. 15, 1969, http://www.aavw.org/served/racetensions_riots_abstract03_full.html.

21. DoD Directive 1350.2, "Department of Defense Military Equal Opportunity (MEO) Program," August 2, 1995; Army AR 600-20, "Army Command Policy," Chapter 6 and App. D; Navy SECNAVINST 5354.1, "Policy on Military Equal Opportunity Complaint Processing;" Marine Corps MCO P5354.1D, "Marine Corps Equal Opportunity (EO) Manual;" Air Force AFI 36-2706, "Military Equal Opportunity Program."

Chapter 6: Sexual Harassment and Sexual Assault in the Military

1. Not in Our Name, *International Commission of Inquiry on Crimes against Humanity Committed by the Bush Administration*, www.bushcommission.org.

2. Rick Maze, "Senator: DoD Must Eliminate Sexual Assaults,"

Navy Times, July 12, 2008, reporting on response to figures released by the Department of Defense Sexual Assault Prevention and Response Office.

3. Brenda Farrell, Director of Defense Capabilities and Management, Government Accountability Office, "Military Personnel: Preliminary Observations on DoD's Sexual Assault Prevention and Response Programs," GAO-08-1013T, July 31, 2008.

4. Rachel N. Lipari and others, *2006 Gender Relations Survey of Active Duty Members* (Arlington, VA: Defense Manpower Data Center, 2008), http://www.sapr.mil/contents/references/WGRA_Overview Report.pdf.

5. Lolita Baldor, "Survey: 6 in 10 Military Women Harassed," *Associated Press,* Sept. 29, 2005.

6. Cortright, *Soldiers in Revolt,* 167.

7. Ibid., 170.

8. "Little Known Program: Equal Opportunity Must Be Accorded Women," *Commander's Digest* 12, no. 2 (May 18, 1972), 5.

9. Helen Benedict, "The Private War of Women Soldiers," *Salon.com,* March 7, 2007. http://www.salon.com/news/feature/2007/03/07/women_in_military.

10. House Committee on Armed Services, *Women in the Military: The Tailhook Affair and the Problem of Sexual Harassment,* 102nd Cong., 2nd sess., 1992. (Hereafter, *Tailhook Report.*)

11. Associated Press, "Rumsfeld orders investigation into reports of sexual assaults," Feb. 6, 2004.

12. Department of Defense Care for Victims of Sexual Assault Task Force, *Task Force Report on Care for Victims of Sexual Assault,* April 2004.

13. Miles Moffeit and Amy Herdy, "For Crime Victims, Punishment," *Denver Post,* November 16, 2003.

14. Army AR 600-20, "Army Command Policy," Chapter 8; Navy SECNAVINST 1752.4A "Sexual Assault Prevention And Response;" Marine Corps MCO 1725.5A, "Sexual Assault Prevention and Response Program." (Air force instructions pending.)

Chapter 7: The Medical Side of War

1. Kelly Kennedy, "Wounded and Waiting," *Army Times,* February 20, 2007.

2. Dana Priest and Anne Hull, "'A Soldier's Officer,'" *Washington*

Post, Dec. 2, 2007; Dana Priest, "Soldier Suicides Reach Record Level" *Washington Post*, January 30, 2008.

3. Esther Schrader, "These Unseen Wounds Cut Deep," *Los Angeles Times*, November 14, 2004.

4. Rone Tempest, "Bloody Scenes Haunt a Marine," *Los Angeles Times*, May 29, 2006.

5. Charles W. Hoge and others, "Combat Duty in Iraq and Afghanistan, Mental Health Problems, and Barriers to Care," *New England Journal of Medicine* 351 (2004): 13–22.

6. Julian E. Barnes, "U.S. Veterans Struggle with War Stress," *Los Angeles Times*, April 18, 2008.

7. Shankar Vedantam, "Veterans Report Mental Distress," *Washington Post*, March 1, 2006.

8. Terri Tanielian and Lisa H. Jaycox, eds., *Invisible Wounds of War: Psychological and Cognitive Injuries, Their Consequences, and Services to Assist Recovery* (Santa Monica, CA: RAND Center for Military Health Policy Research, April 17, 2008).

9. Charles W. Hoge and others, "Mild Traumatic Brain Injury in U.S. Soldiers Returning from Iraq," *New England Journal of Medicine* 358, no. 5 (2008): 453–463.

10. Ronald Glasser, "A Shock Wave of Brain Injuries," *Washington Post*, April 8, 2007.

11. "The Veteran Suicide Epidemic," CBS News, November 13, 2007.

12. *Veterans for Common Sense v. Peake*, 563 F.Supp.2d 1049 (N.D.Cal. 2008).

13. "The Veteran Suicide Epidemic."

14. Chris Adams, "Suicide Shocks Montana into Assessing Vets' Care," *McClatchy Newspapers*, December 28, 2007, http://www.mc clatchydc.com/100/story/23867.html.

15. *Veterans for Common Sense* 563 F.Supp.2d at 1063.

16. "Most Vet Suicides among Guard, Reserve Troops," *Associated Press*, February 12, 2008.

17. Kimberly Hefling, "A Soldier's Suicide: Did He Have to Die?" *Associated Press*, December 20, 2007.

18. DoD Instruction 1332.14, "Enlisted Administrative Separations," Encl 3.A1.3.a.(8), August 28, 2008.

19. Maya Schenwar and Matt Renner, "Veterans Attest to PTSD Neglect by VA," *Truthout*, May 12, 2008, http://www.truthout.org/article/veterans-attest-ptsd-neglect-va.

20. Dana Priest and Anne Hull, "Soldiers Face Neglect, Frustration at Army's Top Medical Facility," *Washington Post*, February 18, 2007.

21. Department of Defense and Department of Veterans Affairs, *Preliminary Observations on Efforts to Improve Health Care and Disability Evaluations for Returning Servicemembers*, April 2007, http://www.gao.gov/new.items/d071256t.pdf.

22. Gregg Zoroya, "U.S. Deploys More Than 43,000 Unfit for Combat," *USA Today*, April 7, 2008.

23. Erin Emery, "Ailing GIs Deployed to War Zone," *Denver Post*, January 17, 2008.

24. "Soldier, After Bipolar Treatment and Suicide Attempts, Sent Back to War Zone," *Associated Press*, February 11, 2008.

25. Lisa Chedekel and Matthew Kauffman, "U.S. Redeploying Troops with Mental Health Issues," *Hartford Courant*, May 14, 2006.

26. Ibid.

27. Lisa Chedekel and Matthew Kauffman, "Mentally Unfit, Forced to Fight," *Hartford Courant*, May 14, 2006.

28. Matthew Kauffman and Lisa Chedekel, "Slipping through the System," *Hartford Courant*, May 15, 2006.

29. *Ronald Reagan National Defense Authorization Act for Fiscal Year 2005*, 108th Cong., PL 108-375, October 28, 2004.

30. DoD Directive 6025.19, "Individual Medical Readiness," January 3, 2006.

31. Department of Defense, "Policy Guidance for Deployment-Limiting Psychiatric Conditions and Medications," Memorandum, November 7, 2006, mandated by Sec. 738 of the National Defense Authorization Act for Fiscal Year 2007, Public Law 109-364.

32. Mark Thompson, "America's Medicated Army," *Time*, June 5, 2008.

33. Ibid.

34. David M. Benedek, Brett J. Schneider, and John C. Bradley, "Psychiatric Medications for Deployment—an Update," *Military Medicine* 172, no. 7 (July 2007): 681–685.

35. Chedekel and Kauffman, "Mentally Unfit, Forced to Fight."

36. U.S. Government Accountability Office, "Military Personnel—Army Needs to Better Enforce Requirements and Improve Record Keeping for Soldiers Whose Medical Conditions May Call for Significant Duty Limitations," Report to Congressional Requesters, June 2008.

37. DoD Instruction 1332.38, "Physical Disability Evaluation," November 14, 1996.

38. Retirement or Separation for Physical Disability, 10 USC 1201-1221.

39. DoD Instruction 1332.18, "Separation or Retirement for Physical Disability," November 4, 1996; policy is also discussed in DoD Directive 1332.38. The Army regulation is AR 635-40; the Navy and Marine Corps both use SECNAVINST 1850.4.E (the *Navy Manual of the Medical Department*, or MANMED, is also helpful); and the Air Force instruction is AFI 36-3212.

Chapter 8: Discharges

1. DoD Instruction 1332.14, "Enlisted Administrative Separations;" Army Regulation (AR) 635-200; Naval Military Personnel Manual (MILPERSMAN), 1900 series or 1910 series; Marine Corps Separation and Retirement Manual (MARCORSEPMAN), Chapter 6; Air Force Instruction (AFI) 36-3208.

2. DoD Instruction 1332.14, "Enlisted Administrative Separations," Encl. (3), Part E3.3.a.(3).

3. Ibid., Encl. (3), Part E3.8.

4. Army USAREC Regulation 601-56, "Waiver, Future Soldiers Program Separations, and Void Enlistment;" Army USAREC Regulation 601-95, "Delayed Entry and Delayed Training Program;" Marine Corps MCO P1100.72C, "Military Personnel Procurement Manual," Vol. 2, Sec. 4301; Navy MILPERSMAN 1910-136, "Separation from the Delayed Entry Program;" Air Force: AFRSI 36-2001, "Recruiting Procedures for the Air Force;" Air Force AFRSI 36-3209, "Separation and Retirement Procedures for Air National Guard and Air Force Reserve Members."

Chapter 9: The Families

1. Rose Hoban, "The Impact of War: Report: Strained Military Resulting in Abuse, Neglect," National Public Radio, December 17, 2008, http://www.npr.org/templates/story/story.php?storyId=12385667.

2. Dana Milbank, "Putting Her Foot Down and Getting the Boot," *Washington Post*, July 10, 2008; "Former Arlington National Cemetery Public Affairs Director Says She Was Fired for Refusing to Limit Press at Funerals," *DemocracyNow!*, July 23, 2008.

3. Blog comment to Milbank, "Putting Her Foot Down."

4. Kevin B. Zeese, "Honor Our Children's Sacrifices: An Interview with Cindy Sheehan of Gold Star Families for Peace," *Antiwar.com*, May 30, 2005, http://www.antiwar.com/orig/zeese.php?articleid=6133.

5. Cindy Sheehan, Brainy Quote, http://www.brainyquote.com/quotes/authors/c/cindy_sheehan.html.

6. Bill Mitchell, interview, *Lone Star Iconoclast*, August 11, 2005, http://www.tinyrevolution.com/mt/archives/000589.html.

7. Cindy Sheehan, "Transcript of Pro-Stewart Rally, Apr. 27, 2005," Brown University Wiki, https://wiki.brown.edu/confluence/display/MarkTribe/Sheehan+Speeches.

8. Zeese, "Honor Our Children's Sacrifices."

9. Jane Collins, ed., *For Love of a Soldier—Interviews with Military Families Taking Action against the Iraq War* (Boulder, CO: Lexington Books, 2008), 3. All quotations in this section come from *For Love of a Soldier.*

10. Ibid., 203.

11. Ibid., 179, 181.

12. Fernando Suarez del Solar, Guerrero Azteca Peace Project, http://aztecapp.netrootz.com/.

13. David Potorti, "Seeing Cindy," *Common Dreams NewsCenter*, August 12, 2005, http://www.commondreams.org/views05/0812-23.htm.

14. "From One Ground Zero to Another: An Afghan American Who Lost 19 Family Members in U.S. Bombing, and a New Yorker Whose Brother Died in the World Trade Center," *Democracy Now!*, September 11, 2008, http://www.democracynow.org/2008/9/11/from_one_ground_zero_to_another.

15. Bob Herbert, "The Army's Hard Sell," *New York Times*, June 27, 2005.

16. Eduardo Porter, "Army Targets Mom and Pop in Hunt for Hispanic Recruits," *Wall Street Journal*, May 28, 2002.

17. Damien Cave, "Growing Problem for Military Recruiters: Parents," *New York Times*, June 3, 2005.

18. Bob Herbert, "They Won't Go," *New York Times*, June 13, 2005.

Chapter 10: Conclusion

1. Ehren Watada, press conference, Tacoma, Washington, June 7, 2006, quoted in "First Officer Publicly Resists War," marjoriecohn.com, http://marjoriecohn.com/2006/01/first-officer-publicly-resists-war.html.

2. Mejía, *Road from Ar Ramadi*, 23.

3. Michelle Chen, "Home from the Military," *Colorlines*, July/August 2008, http://www.coloredgirls.org/article.php?id=258 and printsafe=1.

4. Joshua Key with Lawrence Hill, *The Deserter's Tale* (New York: Atlantic Monthly Press, 2007), 229.

5. Stan Goff, "Hold On to Your Humanity: An Open Letter to GIs in Iraq," *CounterPunch*, November 15, 2003, http://www.counterpunch.org/goff11142003.html.

6. RAND Corporation, "U.S. Should Rethink 'War On Terrorism' Strategy to Deal with Resurgent Al Qaida," July 29, 2008, http://www.rand.org/news/press/2008/07/29/.

7. Chen, "Home from the Military."

8. Rick Jahnkow, conversation with the authors.

9. Pablo Paredes, conversation with the authors.

10. See GIRadio.org. See also "'Iraq Veterans Against the War' Open Coffeehouse Near Fort Lewis, US," *Indymedia UK*, July 28, 2008, http://www.indymedia.org.uk/en/2008/07/404856.html.

11. "Canadian Parliament Votes to Support War Resisters," Iraq Veterans Against the War, June 3, 2008, http://ivaw.org/ivawupdates?page=3.

12. Aimee Allison and David Solnit, *Army of None: Strategies to Counter Military Recruitment, End War, and Build a Better World* (New York: Seven Stories Press, 2007), xi–xii.

13. Jennifer Hogg, "Military Women Ready to Rock the Boat," *Women's Media Center*, July 18, 2002, http://www.womensmediacenter.com/ex/071808.html.

Index

Acknowledgments

We are grateful to each other for partnering in this awesome project with commitment, dedication, and patience; to our editors, Peter Richardson, Melissa Edeburn, David Peattie, and Mike Mollett; and to our publisher, Scott Jordan, a Vietnam veteran who believes in this book. Thanks also to those who helped us: Christina Becker, Phyllis Bennis, Rick Blumberg, Charles T. Bumer (deceased), Larry Christian, Jan Dauss, Joy Delman, Barbara Dudley, Jim Feldman, Vaughdean Forbes, Peter Goldberger, Karen Hershman, Rudy Hasl, Lori Hurlebaus, Katherine Jashinski, Rick Jahnkow, Kenneth Kagan, Howard Levy, Lori Libs, Jorge Mariscal, Laughlin McDonald, Camilo Mejía, Patrick Meyer, Eric Mitnick, Nancy Cohn Morgan, Christine Mrak, Pablo Paredes, Bruce Pollock, Benjamin Staub, Gilbert Susana, and David Zeiger.

Marjorie thanks her father, Leonard Cohn; mother, Florence Cohn; and sons, Victor and Nicolas Cohn-López, for their constant support, and her husband, Jerry Wallingford, for his love and patience.

Kathleen thanks her friends in the Military Law Task Force for putting up with her during this process, and Aaron Frishberg, Lynn Gonzalez, Jeoffry Gordon, and Ava Torre-Bueno for sharing their strength with her. She particularly thanks her coauthor for her encouragement and support.

About the Authors

A veteran of the anti–Vietnam War movement, **MARJORIE COHN** is president of the National Lawyers Guild and a professor at Thomas Jefferson School of Law. She is a prominent scholar and lecturer, author of *Cowboy Republic: Six Ways the Bush Gang Has Defied the Law*, and coauthor of *Cameras in the Courtroom: Television and the Pursuit of Justice*. A graduate of Stanford University and Santa Clara University School of Law, Professor Cohn is a criminal defense attorney who publishes in the academic and popular press about criminal justice, U.S. foreign policy and human rights, and she provides commentary for local, regional, national, and international media. She testifies as an expert witness on the illegality of the wars in military courts-martial. Her articles are archived at her Web site, marjoriecohn.com.

KATHLEEN GILBERD is a veteran of the antiwar movement as well, having been involved in support work for the GI movement and military counseling since 1971. As a paralegal she has worked on groundbreaking cases on HIV discrimination in the military and participated in the legal teams representing Pablo Paredes, a Navy war resister; Margarethe Cammermeyer, an Army colonel who won reinstatement after discharge for homosexuality; Ben Sasway, the first draft registration resister prosecuted in the1980s; and a wide range of cases challenging discriminatory military policies. Ms. Gilberd is cochair of the National Lawyers Guild's Military Law Task Force and a frequent contributor to its legal publication, *On Watch*. She serves on the national advisory committee for the GI Rights Network. She has a BA in sociology from the University of California and has completed the California law office study program, an alternative to law school.

Other Books from PoliPointPress

The Blue Pages: A Directory of Companies Rated by Their Politics and Practices
Helps consumers match their buying decisions with their political values by listing
the political contributions and business practices of over 1,000 companies. $9.95,
paperback.

Rose Aguilar, *Red Highways: A Liberal's Journey into the Heartland*
Challenges red state stereotypes to reveal new strategies for progressives. $15.95,
paperback.

Dean Baker, *Plunder and Blunder: The Rise and Fall of the Bubble Economy*
Chronicles the growth and collapse of the stock and housing bubbles and
explains how policy blunders and greed led to the catastrophic—but completely
predictable—market meltdowns. $15.95, paperback.

Jeff Cohen, *Cable News Confidential: My Misadventures in Corporate Media*
Offers a fast-paced romp through the three major cable news channels—Fox CNN,
and MSNBC—and delivers a serious message about their failure to cover the most
urgent issues of the day. $14.95, paperback.

Marjorie Cohn, *Cowboy Republic: Six Ways the Bush Gang Has Defied
the Law*
Shows how the executive branch under President Bush has systematically defied the
law instead of enforcing it. $14.95, paperback.

Marjorie Cohn and Kathleen Gilberd, *Rules of Disengagement:
The Politics and Honor of Military Dissent*
Examines what U.S. military men and women have done—and what their
families and others can do—to resist illegal wars, as well as military racism, sexual
harassment, and denial of proper medical care. $14.95, paperback.

Joe Conason, *The Raw Deal: How the Bush Republicans Plan to Destroy
Social Security and the Legacy of the New Deal*
Reveals the well-financed and determined effort to undo the Social Security Act
and other New Deal programs. $11.00, paperback.

Kevin Danaher, Shannon Biggs, and Jason Mark, *Building the Green
Economy: Success Stories from the Grassroots*
Shows how community groups, families, and individual citizens have protected
their food and water, cleaned up their neighborhoods, and strengthened their local
economies. $16.00, paperback.

Kevin Danaher and Alisa Gravitz, *The Green Festival Reader: Fresh Ideas
from Agents of Change*
Collects the best ideas and commentary from some of the most forward green
thinkers of our time. $15.95, paperback.

Reese Erlich, *Dateline Havana: The Real Story of U.S. Policy and the
Future of Cuba*
Explores Cuba's strained relationship with the United States, the island nation's
evolving culture and politics, and prospects for U.S. Cuba policy with the departure
of Fidel Castro. $22.95, hardcover.

Reese Erlich, *The Iran Agenda: The Real Story of U.S. Policy and the Middle East Crisis*
Explores the turbulent recent history between the two countries and how it has led to a showdown over nuclear technology. $14.95, paperback.

Steven Hill, *10 Steps to Repair American Democracy*
Identifies the key problems with American democracy, especially election practices, and proposes ten specific reforms to reinvigorate it. $11.00, paperback.

Markos Kounalakis and Peter Laufer, *Hope Is a Tattered Flag: Voices of Reason and Change for the Post-Bush Era*
Gathers together the most listened-to politicos and pundits, activists and thinkers, to answer the question: what happens after Bush leaves office? $29.95, hardcover; $16.95 paperback.

Yvonne Latty, *In Conflict: Iraq War Veterans Speak Out on Duty, Loss, and the Fight to Stay Alive*
Features the unheard voices, extraordinary experiences, and personal photographs of a broad mix of Iraq War veterans, including Congressman Patrick Murphy, Tammy Duckworth, Kelly Daugherty, and Camilo Mejia. $24.00, hardcover.

Phillip Longman, *Best Care Anywhere: Why VA Health Care Is Better Than Yours*
Shows how the turnaround at the long-maligned VA hospitals provides a blueprint for salvaging America's expensive but troubled health care system. $14.95, paperback.

Phillip Longman and Ray Boshara, *The Next Progressive Era*
Provides a blueprint for a re-empowered progressive movement and describes its implications for families, work, health, food, and savings. $22.95, hardcover.

Marcia and Thomas Mitchell, *The Spy Who Tried to Stop a War: Katharine Gun and the Secret Plot to Sanction the Iraq Invasion*
Describes a covert operation to secure UN authorization for the Iraq war and the furor that erupted when a young British spy leaked it. $23.95, hardcover.

Susan Mulcahy, ed., *Why I'm a Democrat*
Explores the values and passions that make a diverse group of Americans proud to be Democrats. $14.95, paperback.

David Neiwert, *The Eliminationists: How Hate Talk Radicalized the American Right*
Argues that the conservative movement's alliances with far-right extremists have not only pushed the movement's agenda to the right, but also have become a malignant influence increasingly reflected in political discourse. $16.95, paperback.

Christine Pelosi, *Campaign Boot Camp: Basic Training for Future Leaders*
Offers a seven-step guide for successful campaigns and causes at all levels of government. $15.95, paperback.

William Rivers Pitt, *House of Ill Repute: Reflections on War, Lies, and America's Ravaged Reputation*
Skewers the Bush Administration for its reckless invasions, warrantless wiretaps, lethally incompetent response to Hurricane Katrina, and other scandals and blunders. $16.00, paperback.

Sarah Posner, *God's Profits: Faith, Fraud, and the Republican Crusade for Values Voters*
Examines corrupt televangelists' ties to the Republican Party and unprecedented access to the Bush White House. $19.95, hardcover.

Nomi Prins, *Jacked: How "Conservatives" Are Picking Your Pocket —Whether You Voted for Them or Not*
Describes how the "conservative" agenda has affected your wallet, skewed national priorities, and diminished America—but not the American spirit. $12.00, paperback.

Cliff Schecter, *The Real McCain: Why Conservatives Don't Trust Him— And Why Independents Shouldn't*
Explores the gap between the public persona of John McCain and the reality of this would-be president. $14.95, hardcover.

Norman Solomon, *Made Love, Got War: Close Encounters with America's Warfare State*
Traces five decades of American militarism and the media's all-too-frequent failure to challenge it. $24.95, hardcover.

John Sperling et al., *The Great Divide: Retro vs. Metro America*
Explains how and why our nation is so bitterly divided into what the authors call Retro and Metro America. $19.95, paperback.

Daniel Weintraub, *Party of One: Arnold Schwarzenegger and the Rise of the Independent Voter*
Explains how Schwarzenegger found favor with independent voters, whose support has been critical to his success, and suggests that his bipartisan approach represents the future of American politics. $19.95, hardcover.

Curtis White, *The Spirit of Disobedience: Resisting the Charms of Fake Politics, Mindless Consumption, and the Culture of Total Work*
Debunks the notion that liberalism has no need for spirituality and describes a "middle way" through our red state/blue state political impasse. Includes three powerful interviews with John DeGraaf, James Howard Kunstler, and Michael Ableman. $24.00, hardcover.

For more information, please visit www.p3books.com.